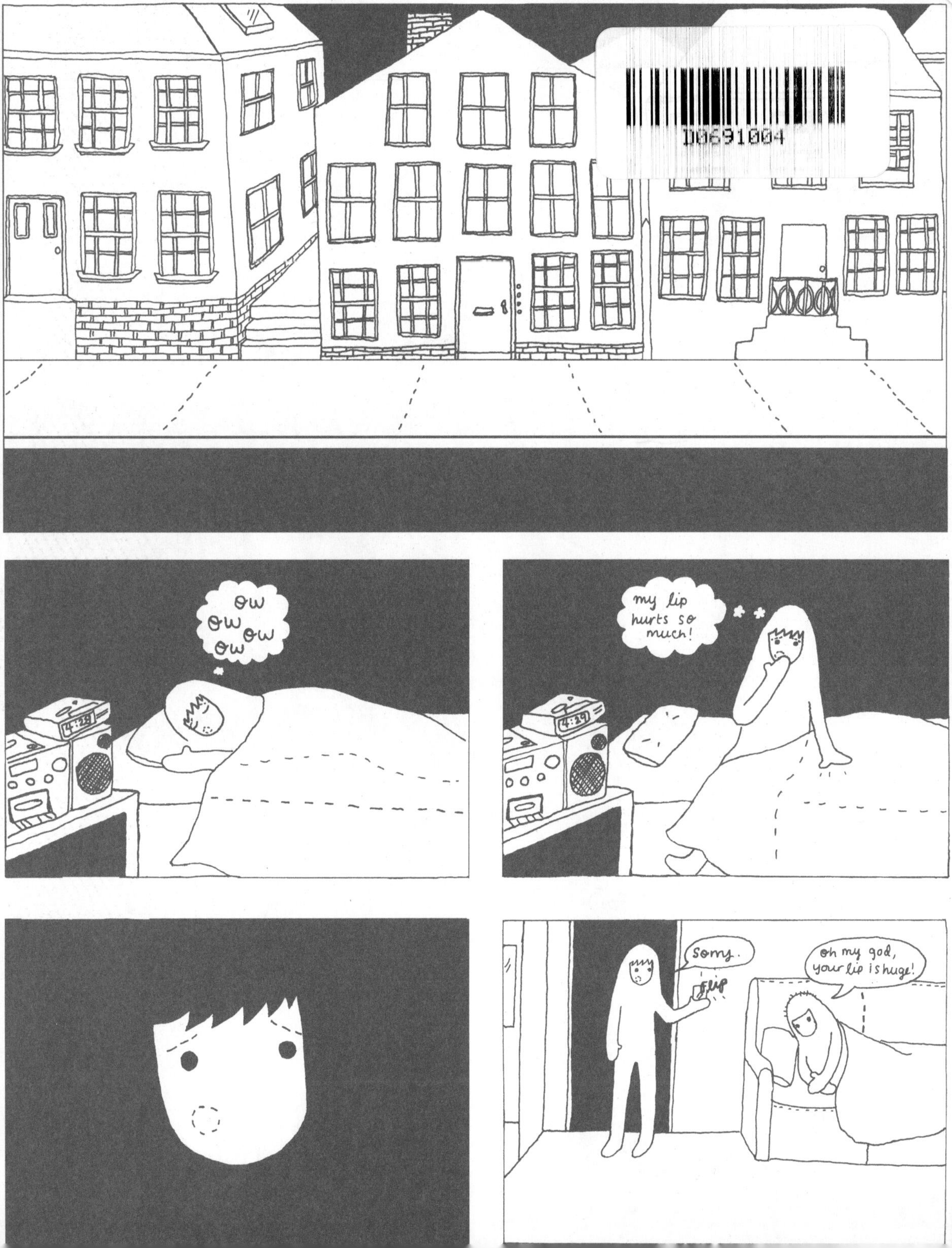
ow ow ow ow
my lip hurts so much!
Sorry.
flip
oh my god, your lip is huge!

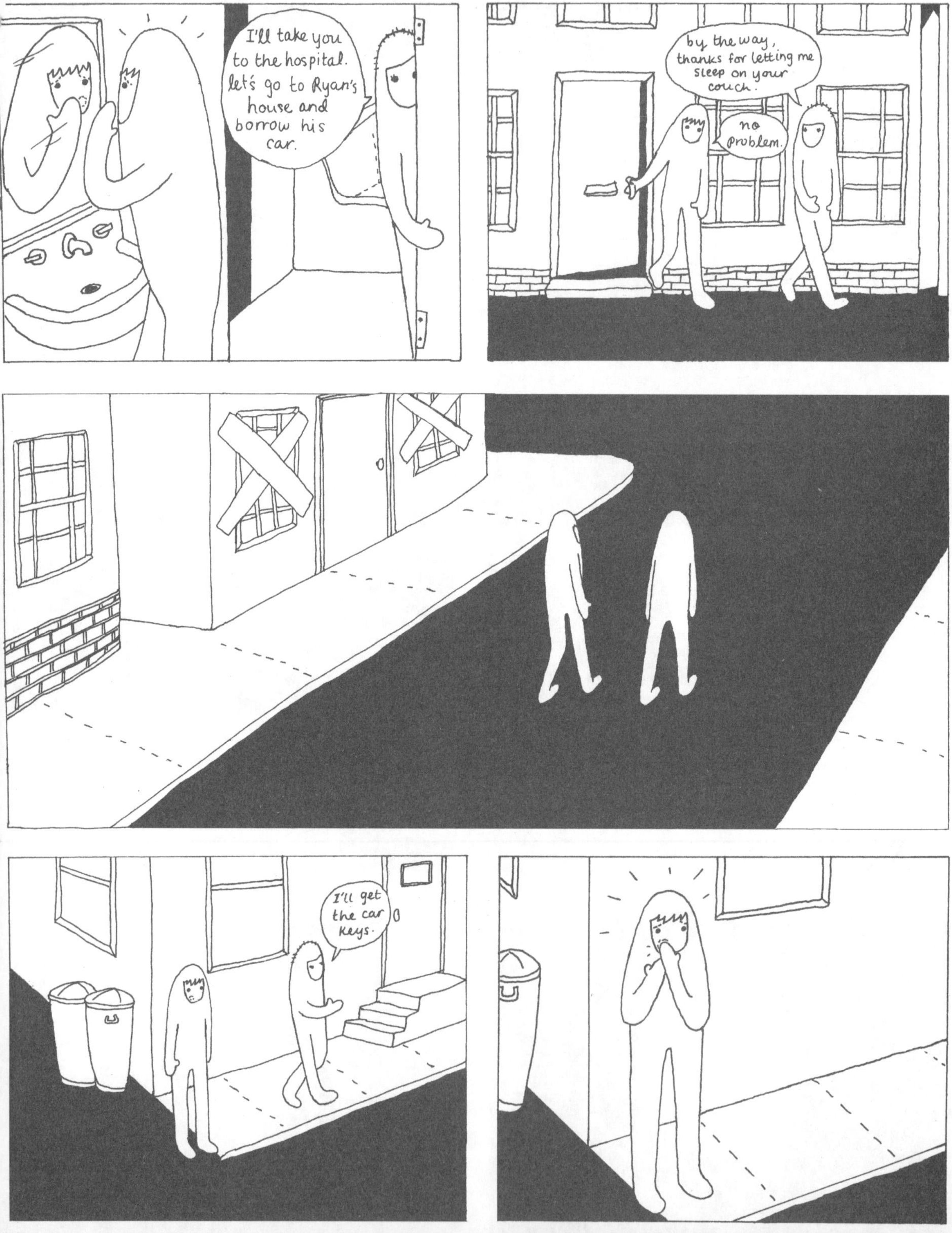
I'll take you to the hospital. let's go to Ryan's house and borrow his car.
by the way, thanks for letting me sleep on your couch.
no problem.
I'll get the car keys.

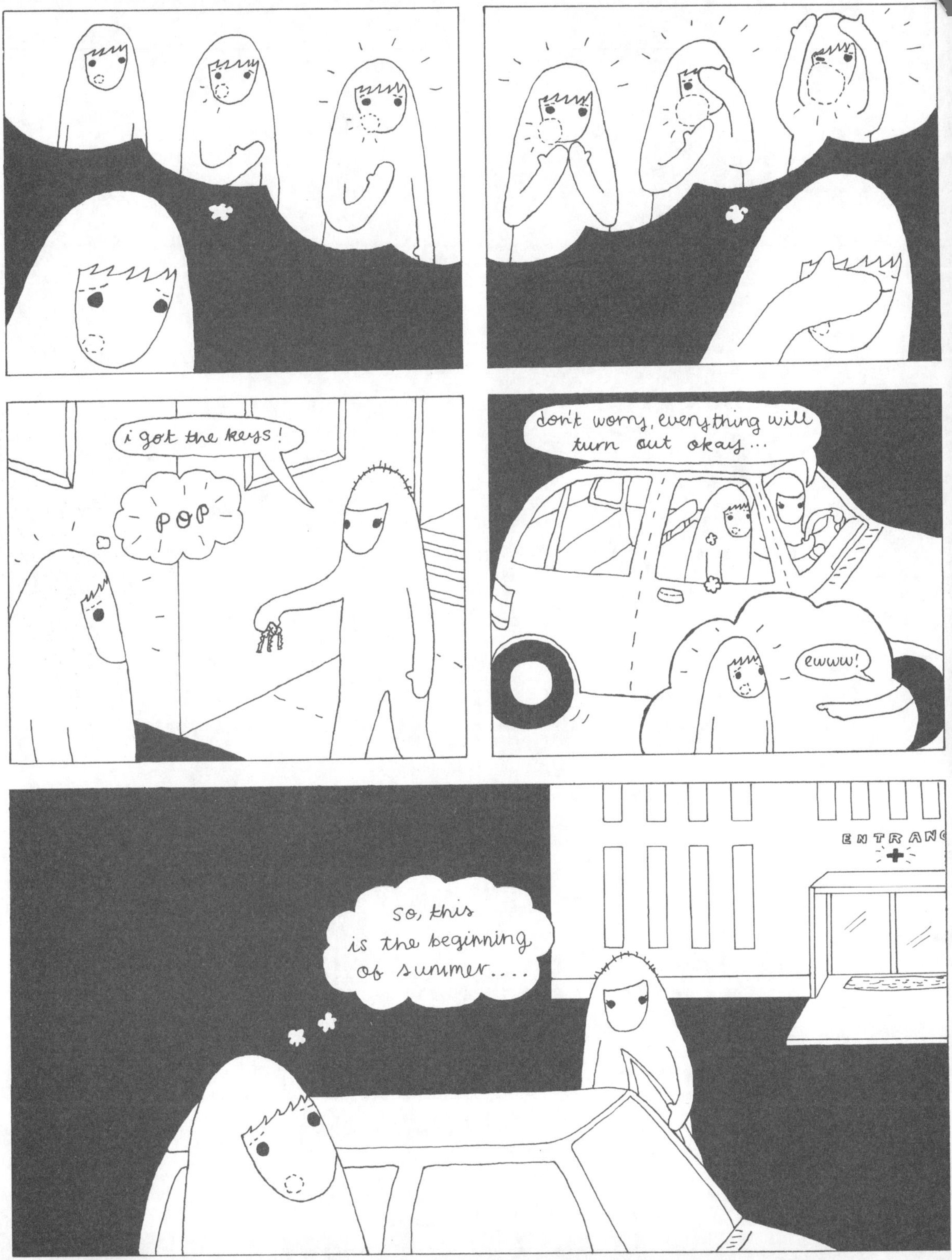
i got the keys!
POP
don't worry, everything will turn out okay...
ewww!
ENTRANC
so, this is the beginning of summer....

never ending summer

allison cole

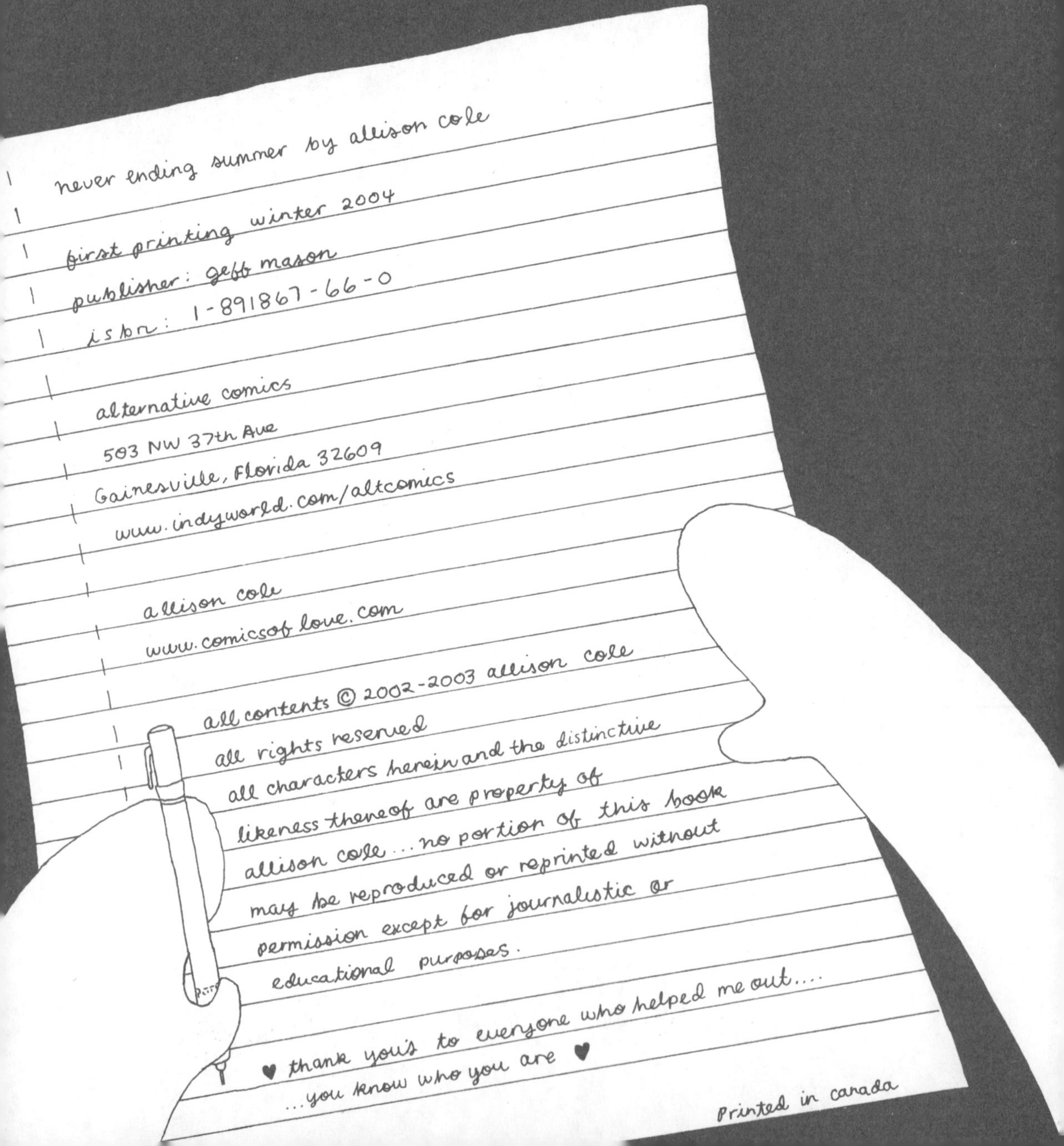

never ending summer by allison cole

first printing winter 2004
publisher: geff mason
isbn: 1-891867-66-0

alternative comics
503 NW 37th Ave
Gainesville, Florida 32609
www.indyworld.com/altcomics

allison cole
www.comicsoflove.com

thank you's to everyone who helped me out....
♥ thank you's to everyone who helped me out.... ♥
...you know who you are

Printed in canada

June

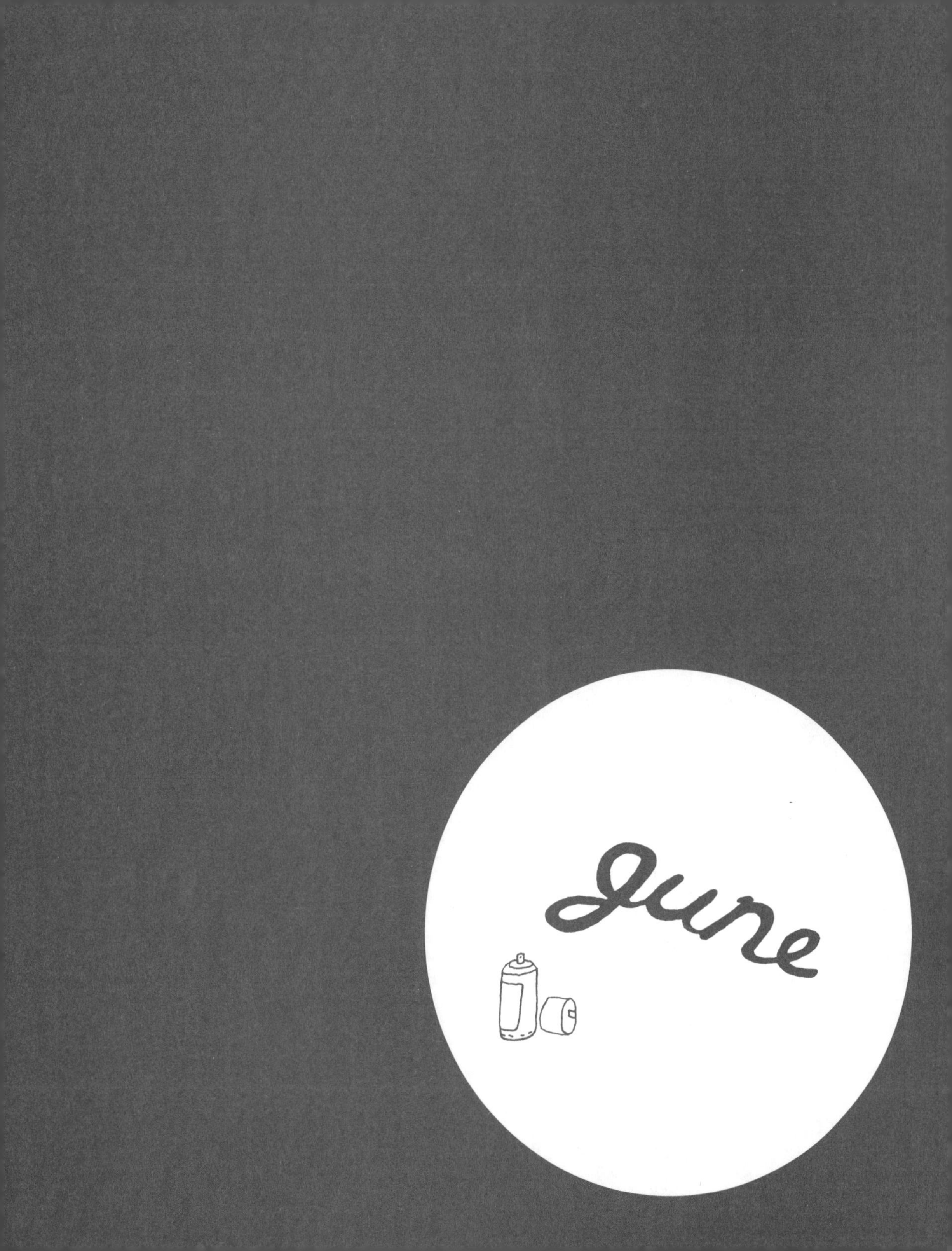

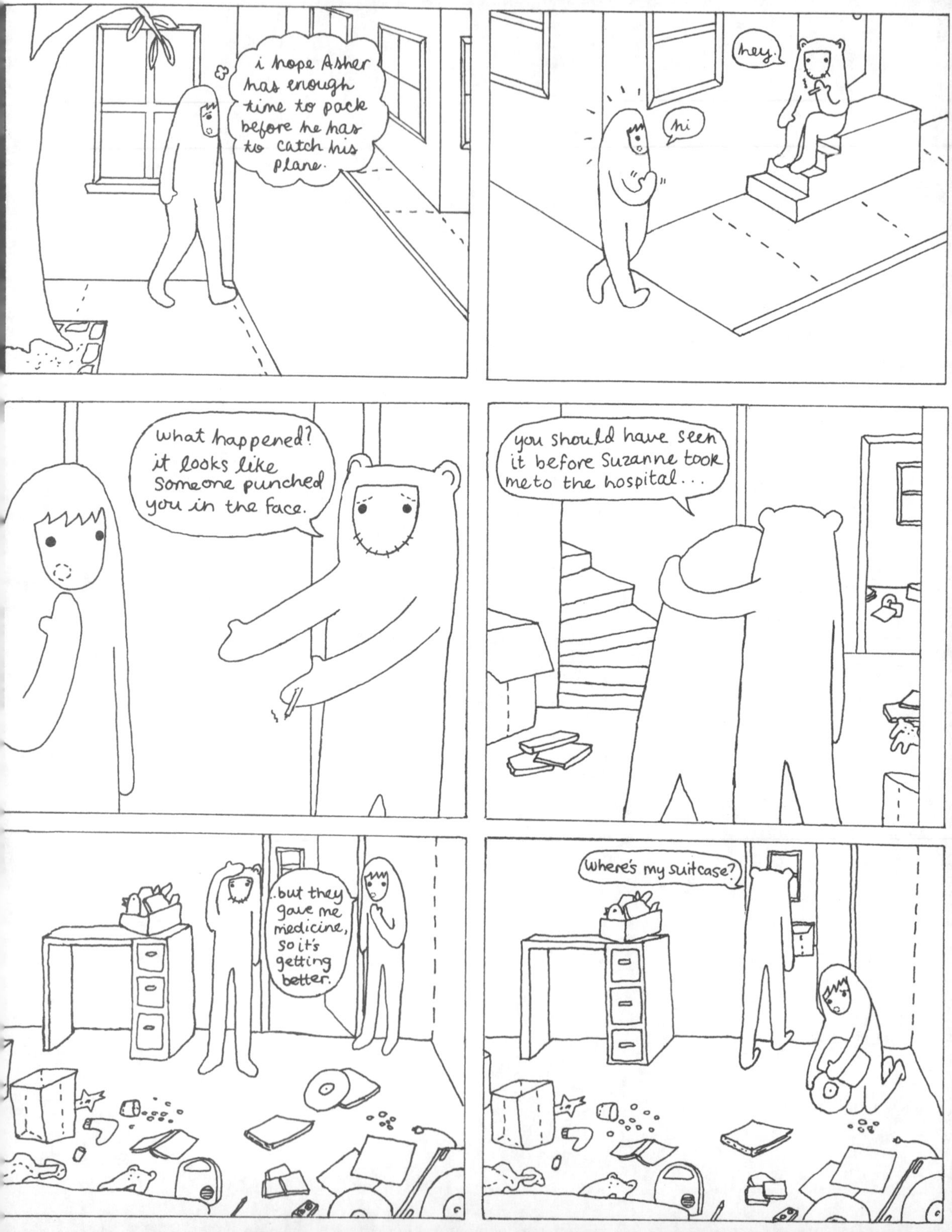
i hope Asher has enough time to pack before he has to catch his plane.
hey.
hi
what happened? it looks like someone punched you in the face.
you should have seen it before Suzanne took me to the hospital...
..but they gave me medicine, so it's getting better.
Where's my suitcase?

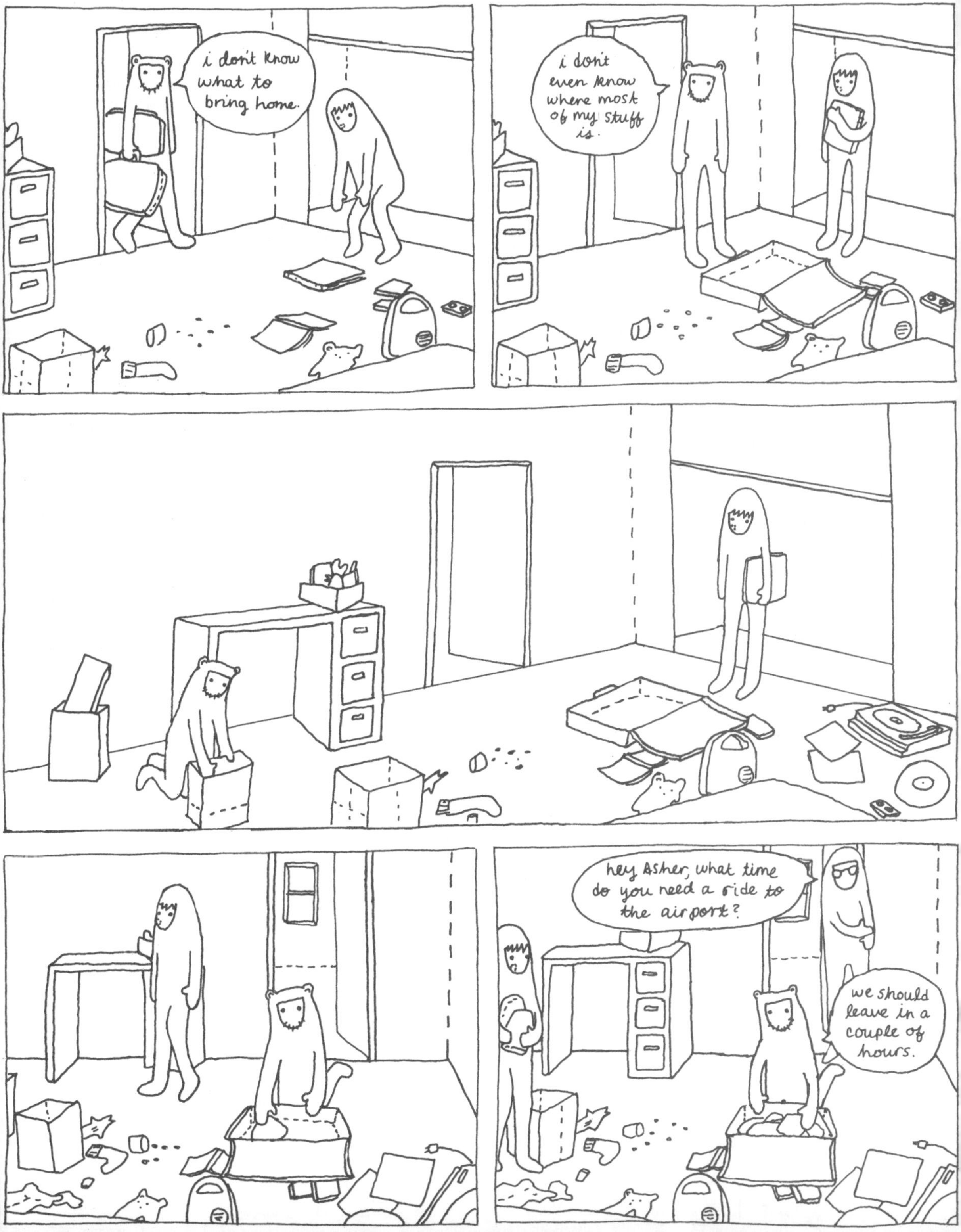
i don't know what to bring home.
i don't even know where most of my stuff is.
hey Asher, what time do you need a ride to the airport?
we should leave in a couple of hours.

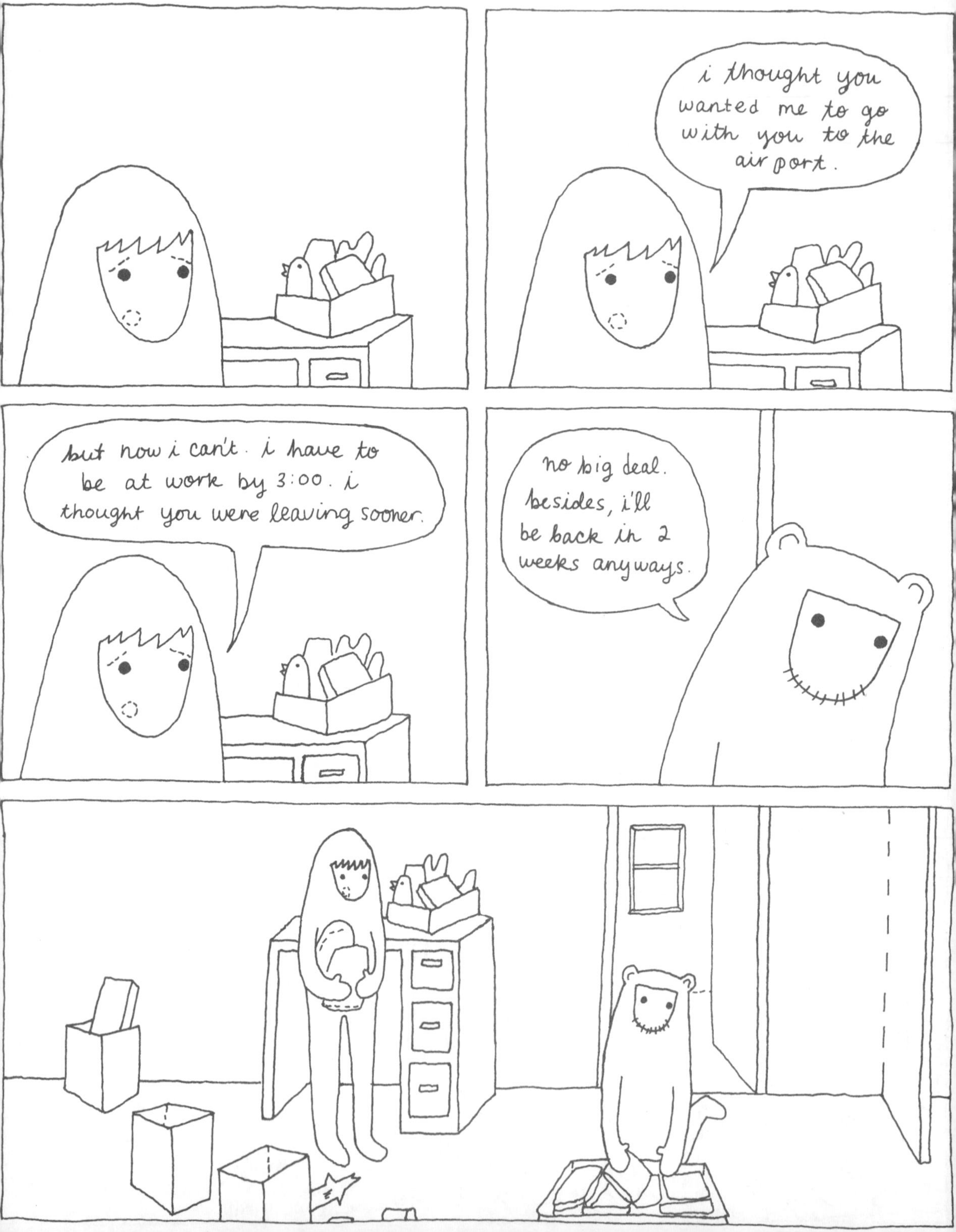
i thought you wanted me to go with you to the air port.
but now i can't. i have to be at work by 3:00. i thought you were leaving sooner.
no big deal. besides, i'll be back in 2 weeks anyways.

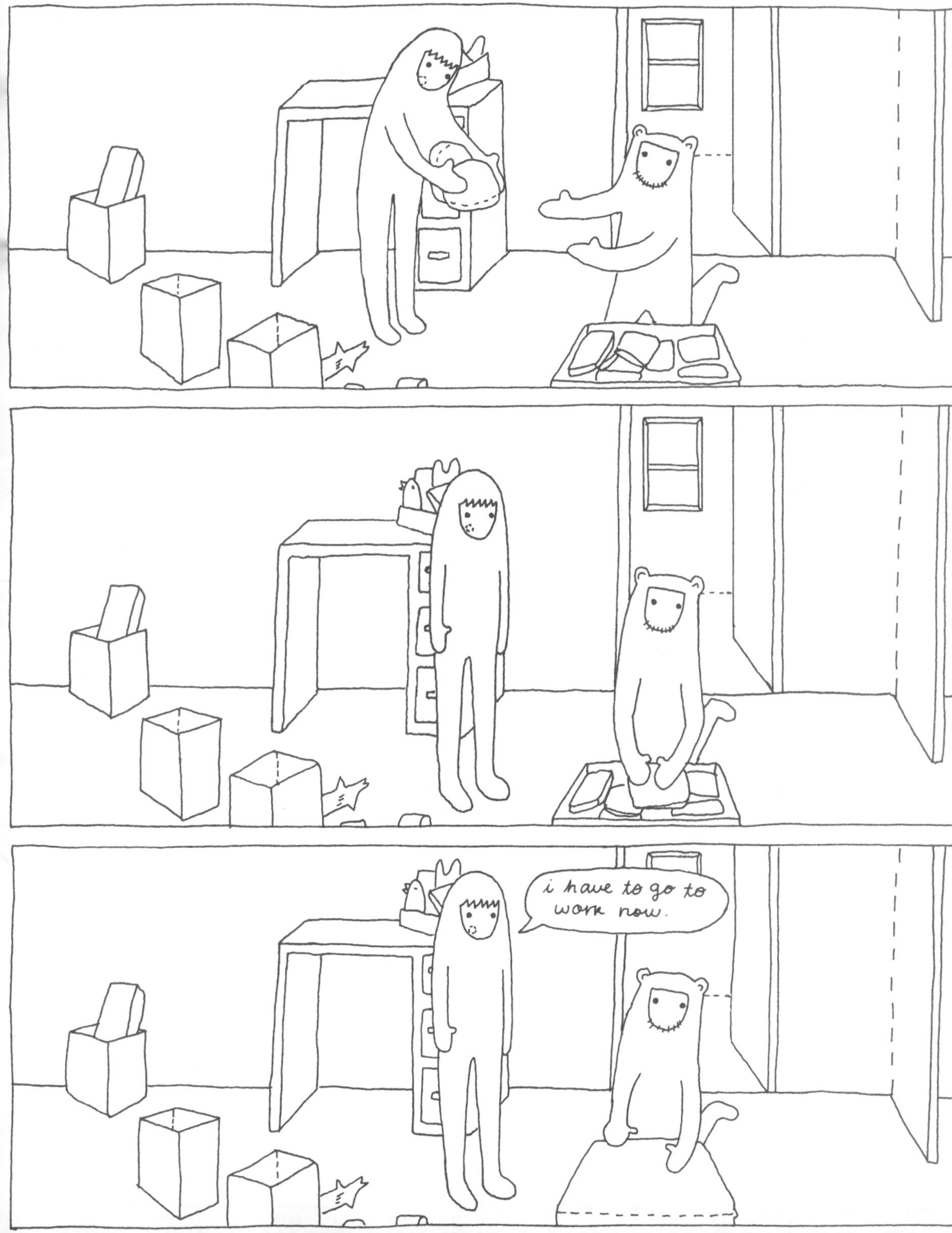
i have to go to work now.

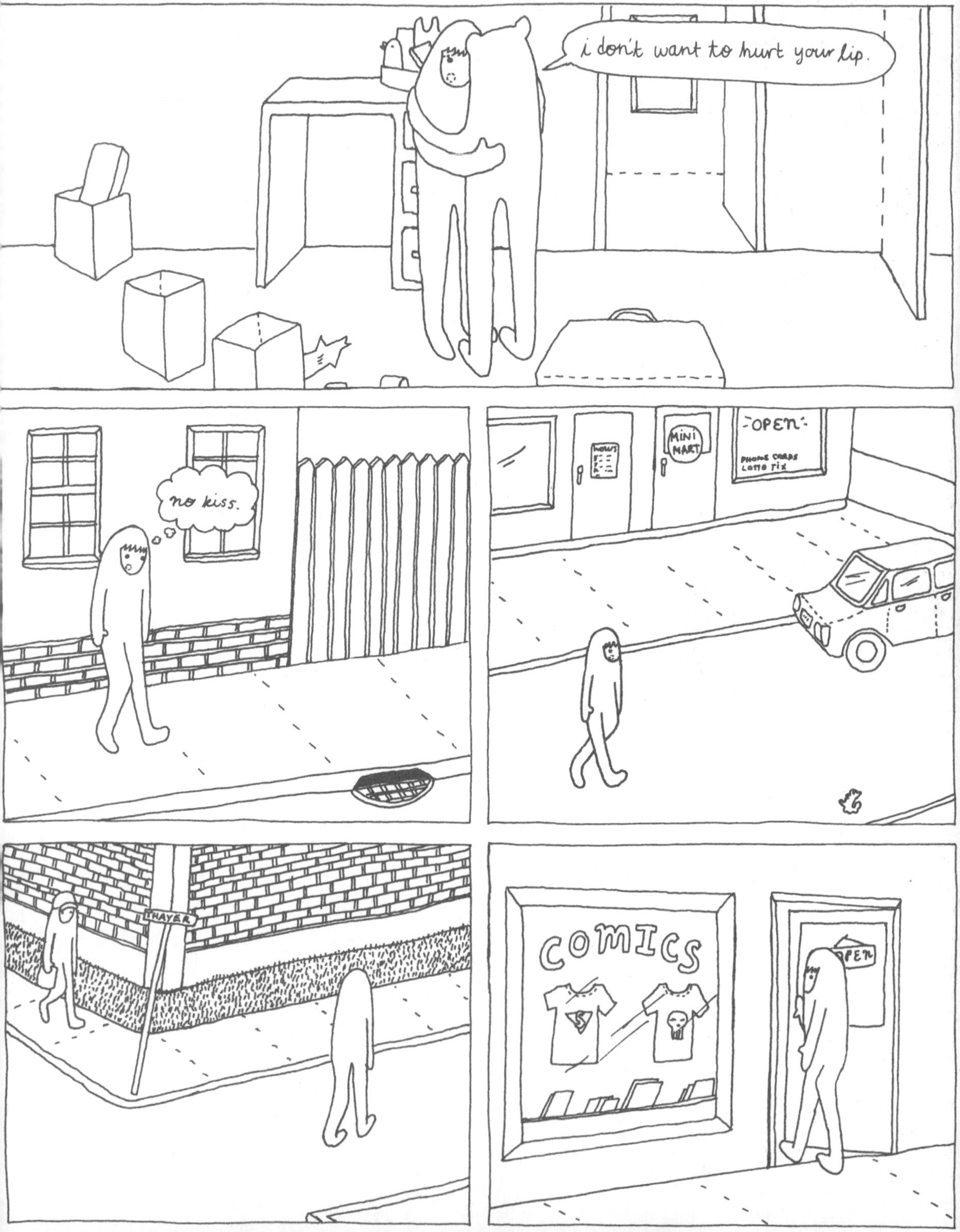
i don't want to hurt your lip.
no kiss.
HOURS
MINI MART
OPEN
PHONE CARDS
LOTTO TIX
THAYER
COMICS

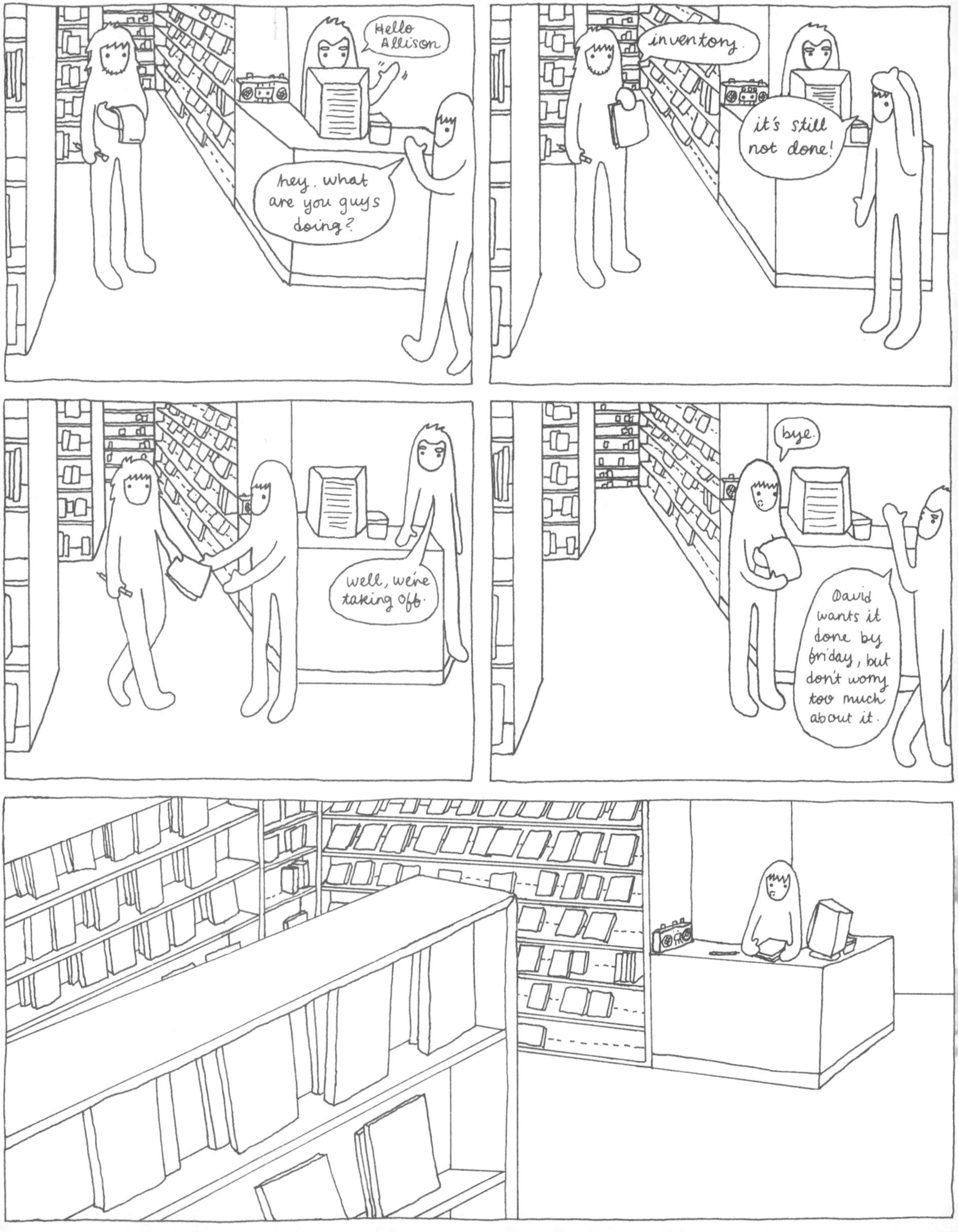
Hello Allison
hey. what are you guys doing?
inventory.
it's still not done!
well, we're taking off.
bye.
David wants it done by friday, but don't worry too much about it.

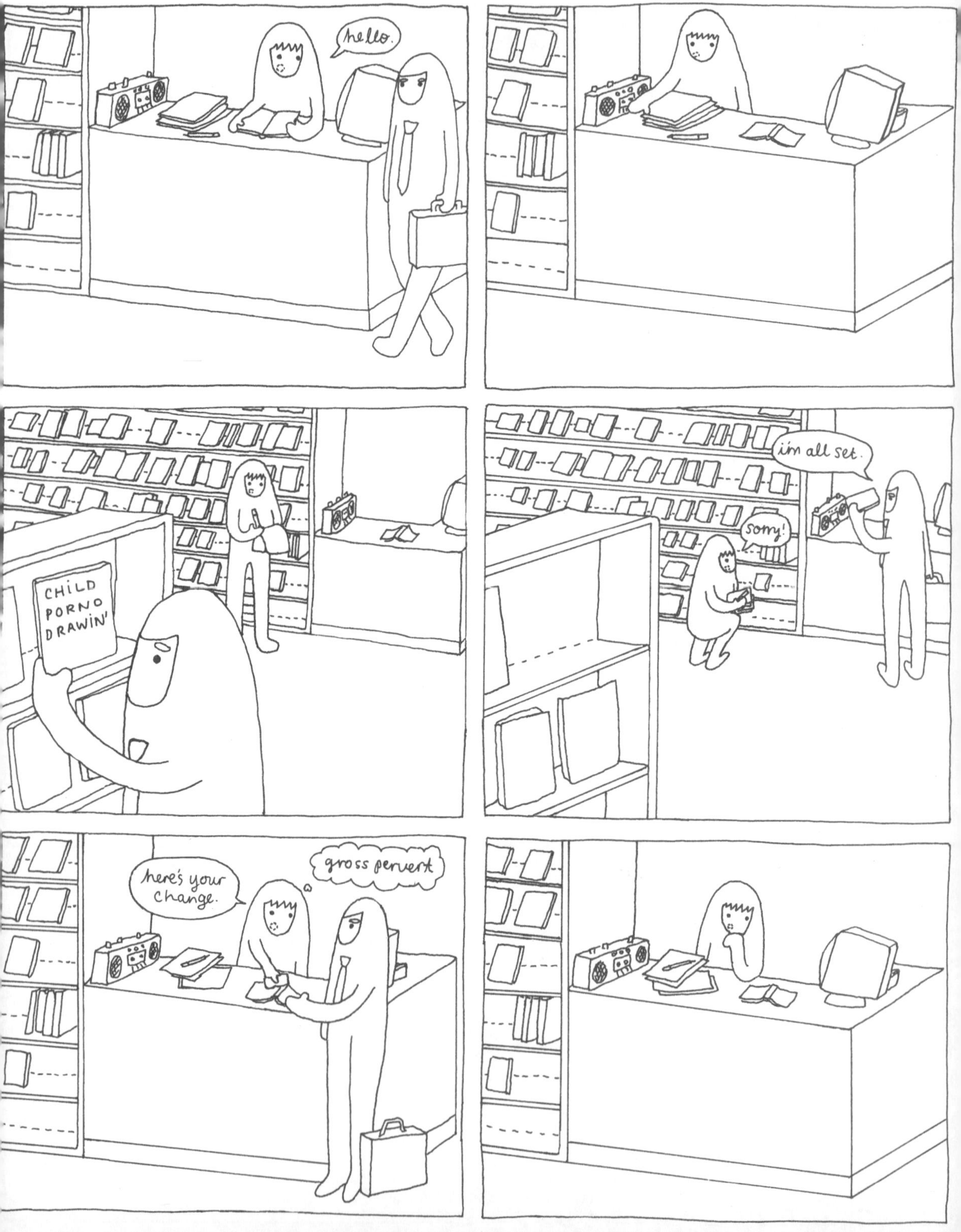
hello.
CHILD PORNO DRAWIN'
i'm all set.
sorry!
here's your change.
gross pervert

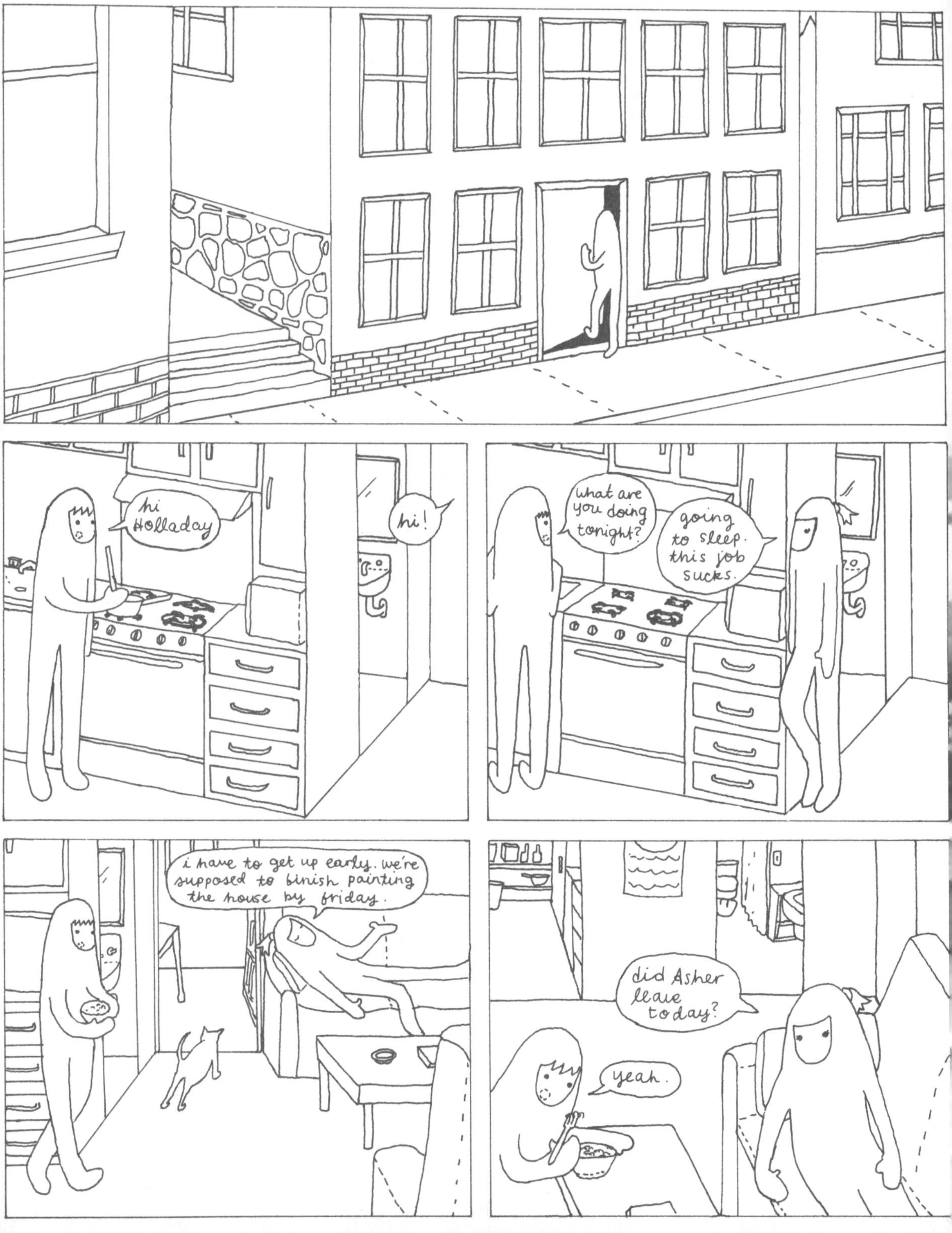
hi Holladay
hi!
what are you doing tonight?
going to sleep. this job sucks.
i have to get up early. we're supposed to finish painting the house by friday.
did Asher leave today?
yeah.

are you going to miss him?
yeah.
i think im going to go stare at my lip in the mirror.
Okay...
good night
night.
why was Asher so weird to me?

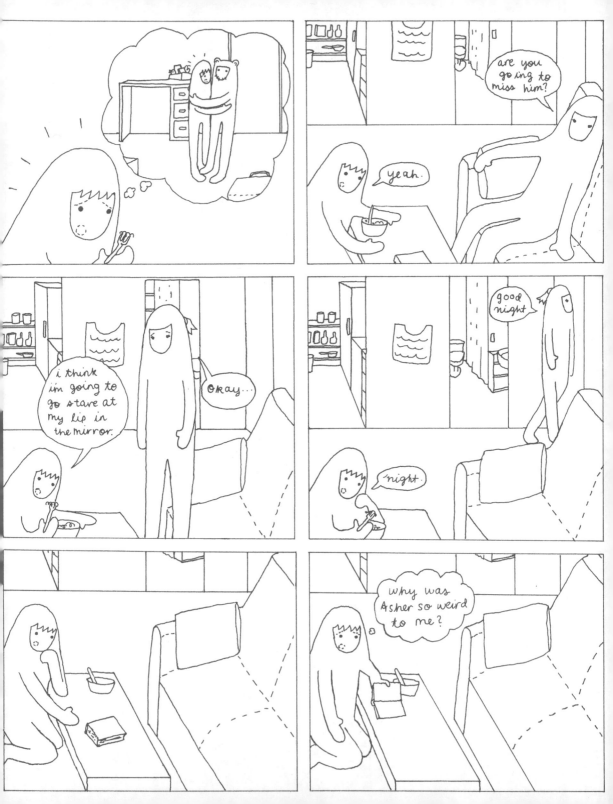

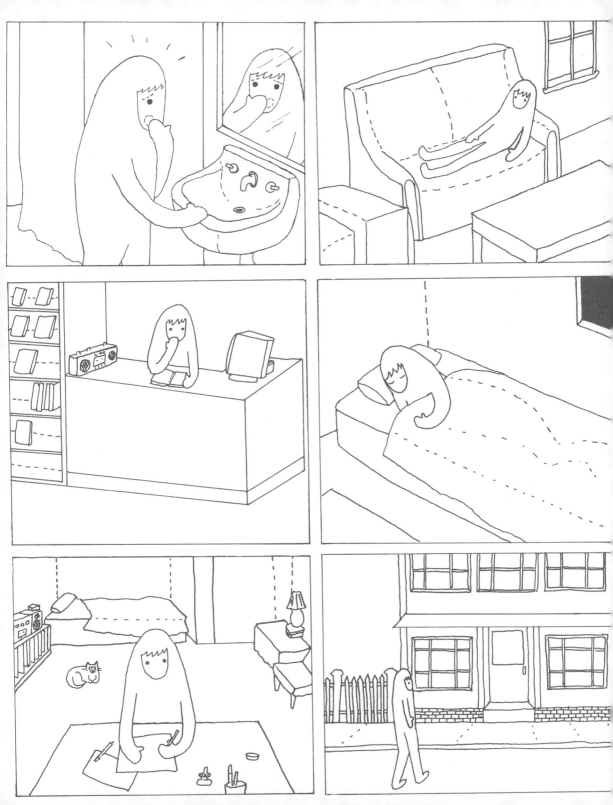

COMICS
OPEN
RING
RING
hello?
hey.
how are you? how's home?
it's great. i met these really nice girls the other day...
and we went to thrift stores to look for toys that i could take photos of...
Oh.

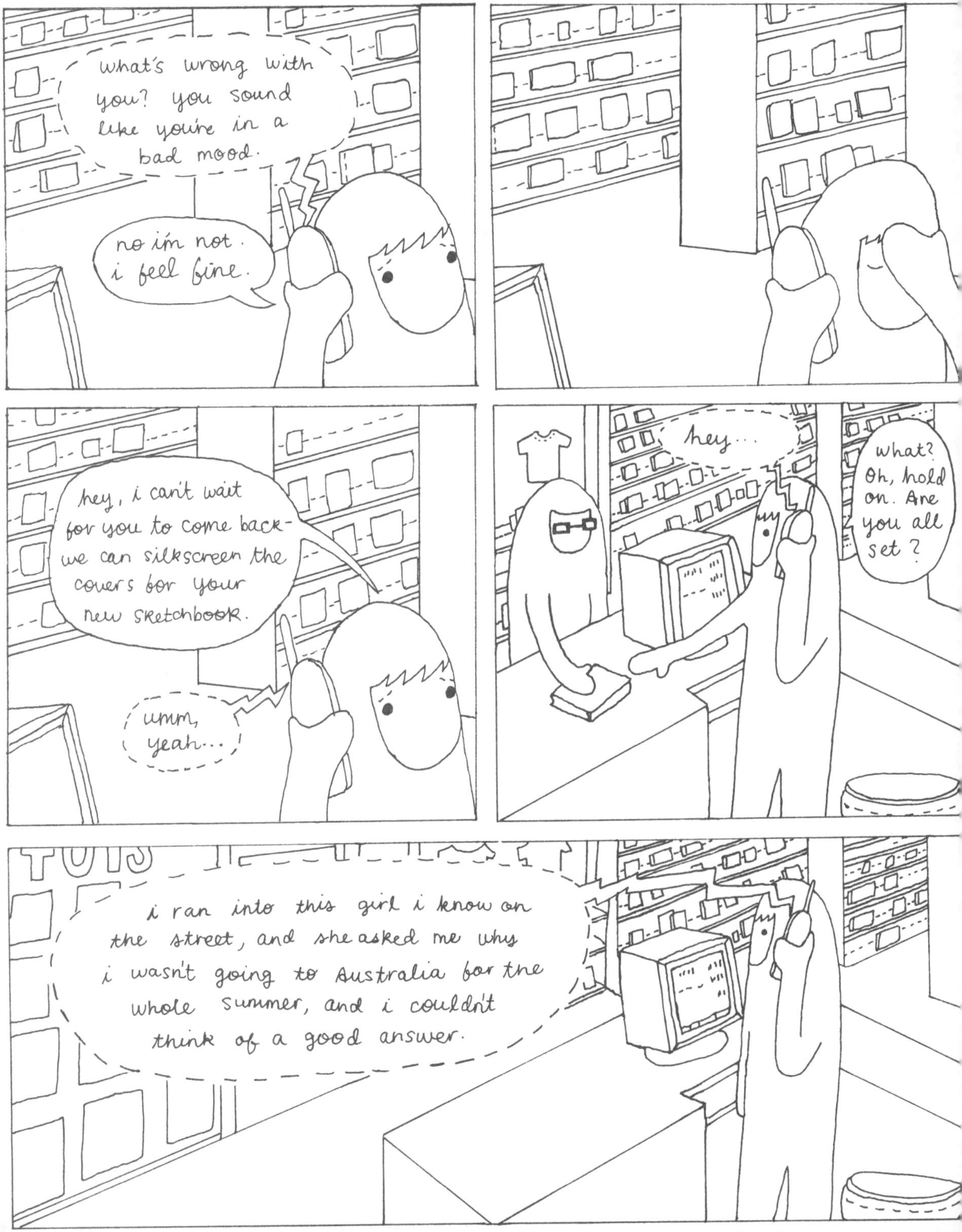
what's wrong with you? you sound like you're in a bad mood.
no i'm not. i feel fine.
hey, i can't wait for you to come back we can silkscreen the covers for your new sketchbook.
umm, yeah...
hey...
what? Oh, hold on. Are you all set?
i ran into this girl i know on the street, and she asked me why i wasn't going to Australia for the whole summer, and i couldn't think of a good answer.

...so, i think im going to go to Australia... instead of coming back to providence.
What? When?
actually, on saturday. im sorry, i just want to have a chance at getting a better internship...
and i can't really think of a good reason why i would want to come back to Providence, except to be with you.

but we had plans for the summer... we were going to do stuff... you were supposed to come back here on saturday.
im sorry.
are you doing this so that you can spend more time with Camille?
Well, this could be a good opportunity to clear things up with her... maybe even... maybe i can get over her.

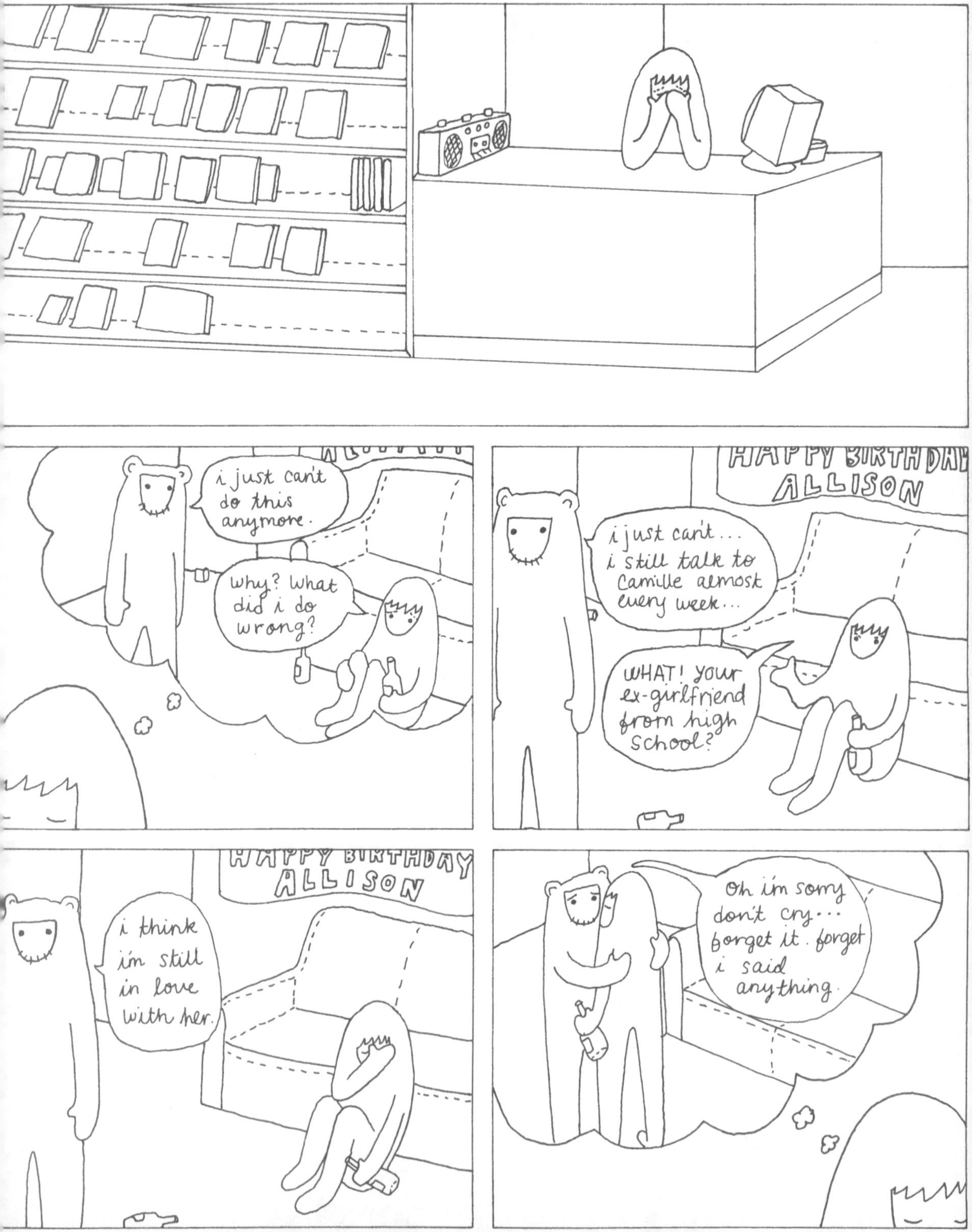
i just can't do this anymore.
why? what did i do wrong?
HAPPY BIRTHDAY ALLISON
i just can't... i still talk to Camille almost every week...
WHAT! your ex-girlfriend from high school?
HAPPY BIRTHDAY ALLISON
i think i'm still in love with her.
Oh i'm sorry don't cry... forget it. forget i said anything.

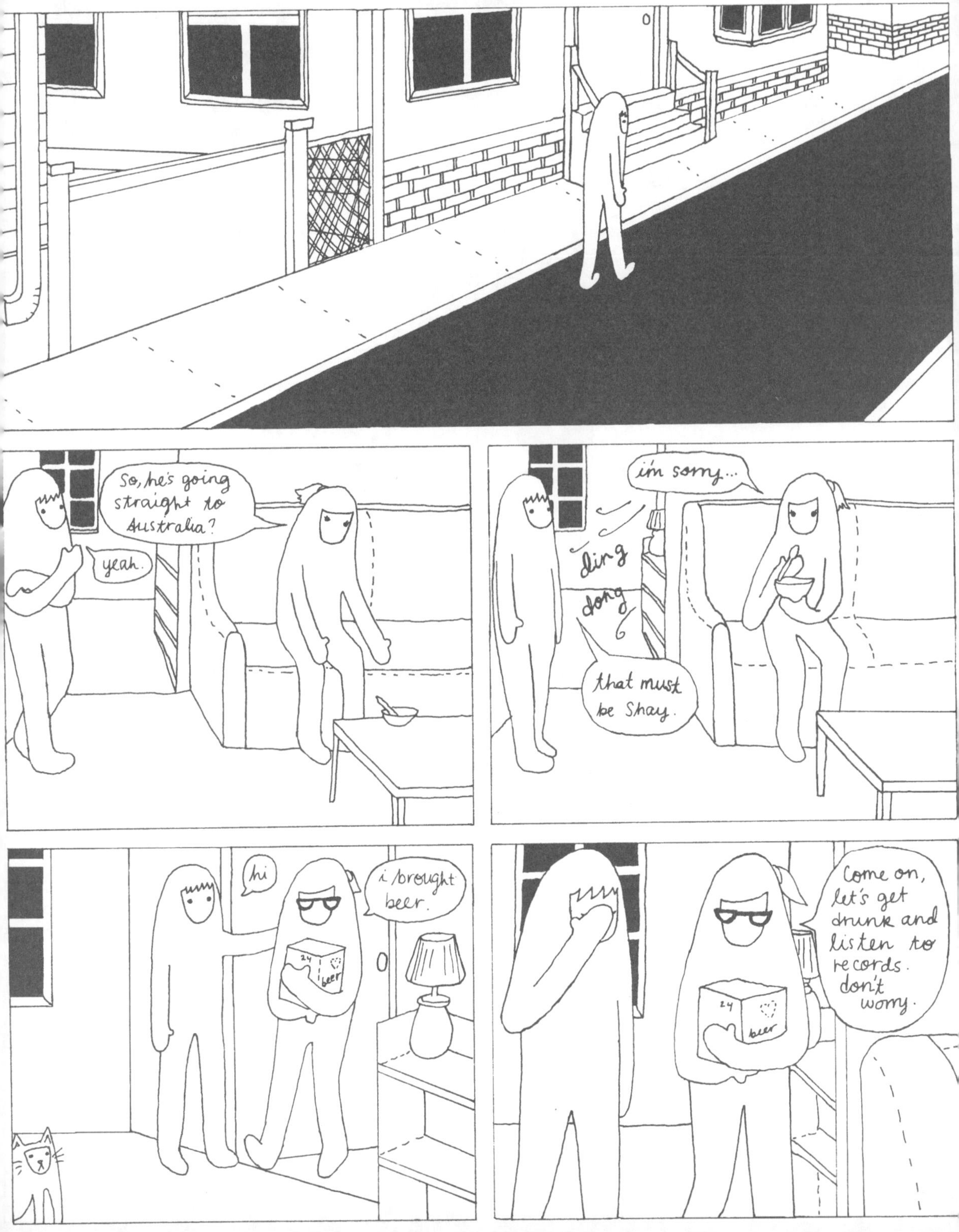

So, he's going straight to Australia?
yeah.
i'm sorry...
ding dong
that must be Shay.
hi
i brought beer.
24
beer
Come on, let's get drunk and listen to records. don't worry.

hi holladay.
hey.
i love this record.
i can't believe he's not coming back!
i'm trying not to worry about it...
i wish will would go away to Australia...
What? Why?
i don't know... i feel like i'm an ant and he's a 12 year old boy on a sunny day with a magnifying glass.

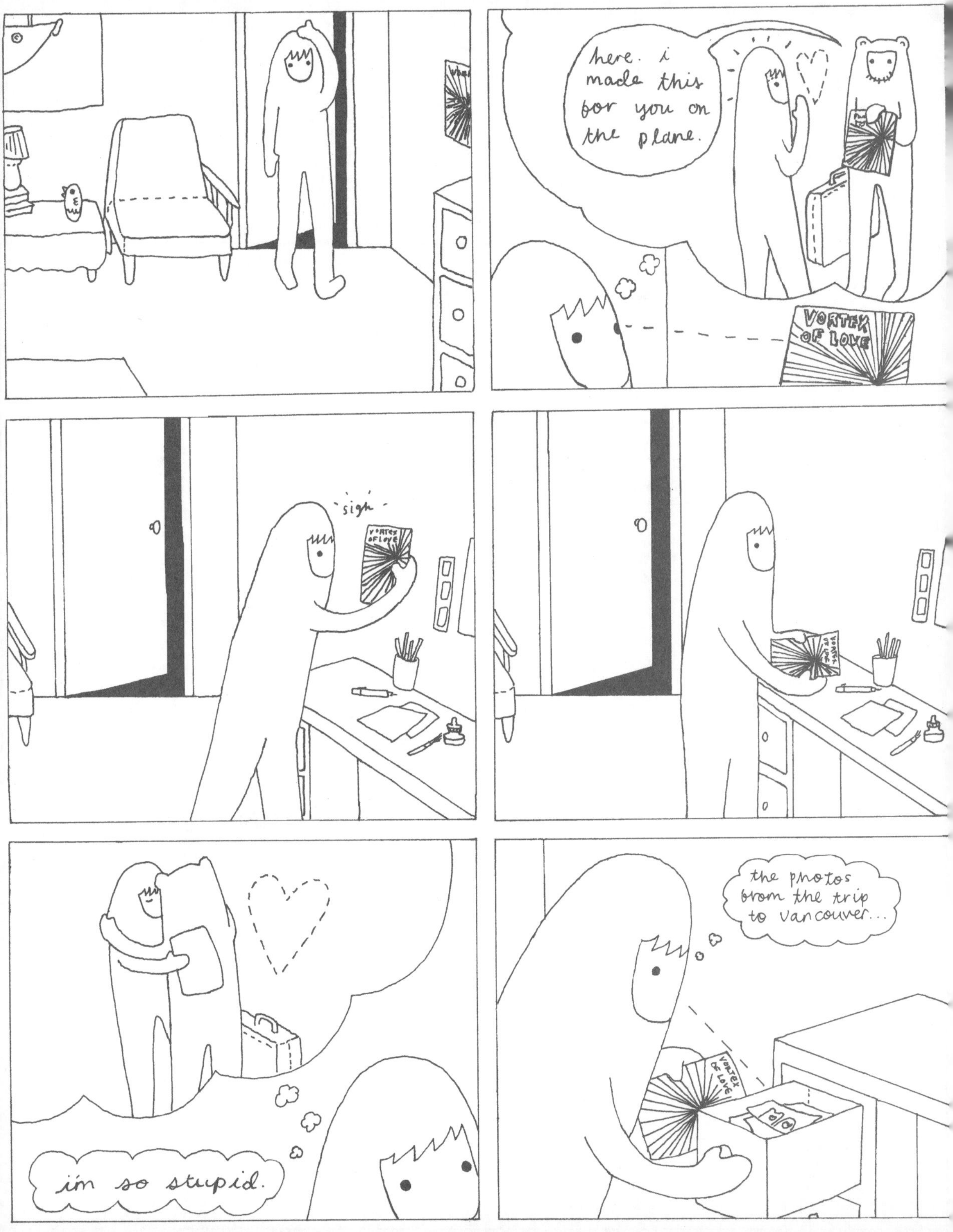
here. i made this for you on the plane.
VORTEX OF LOVE
sigh
VORTEX OF LOVE
im so stupid.
the photos from the trip to vancouver...
VORTEX OF LOVE

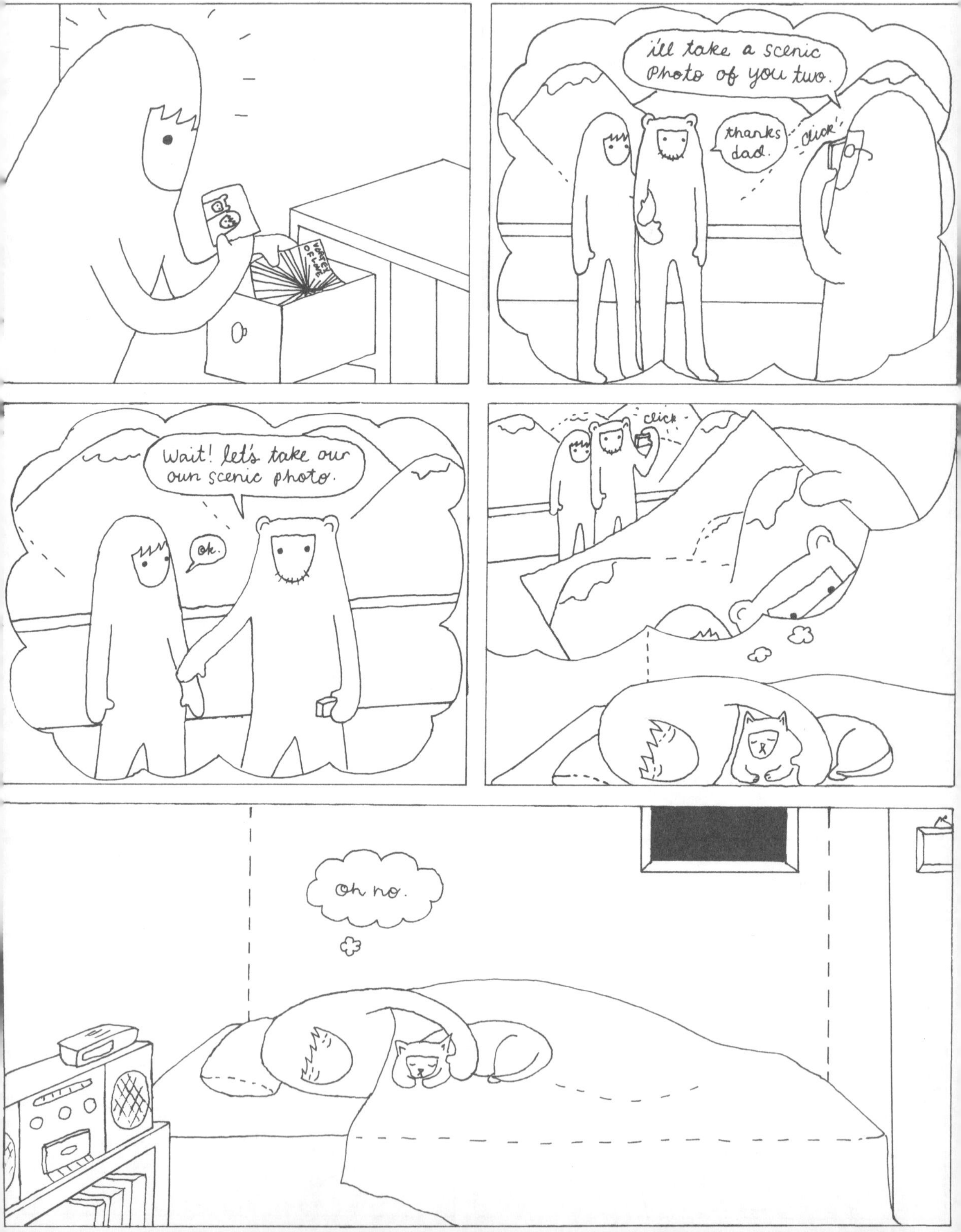
VORTEX OF TIME
i'll take a scenic photo of you two.
thanks dad.
click
Wait! let's take our own scenic photo.
ok.
click
oh no.

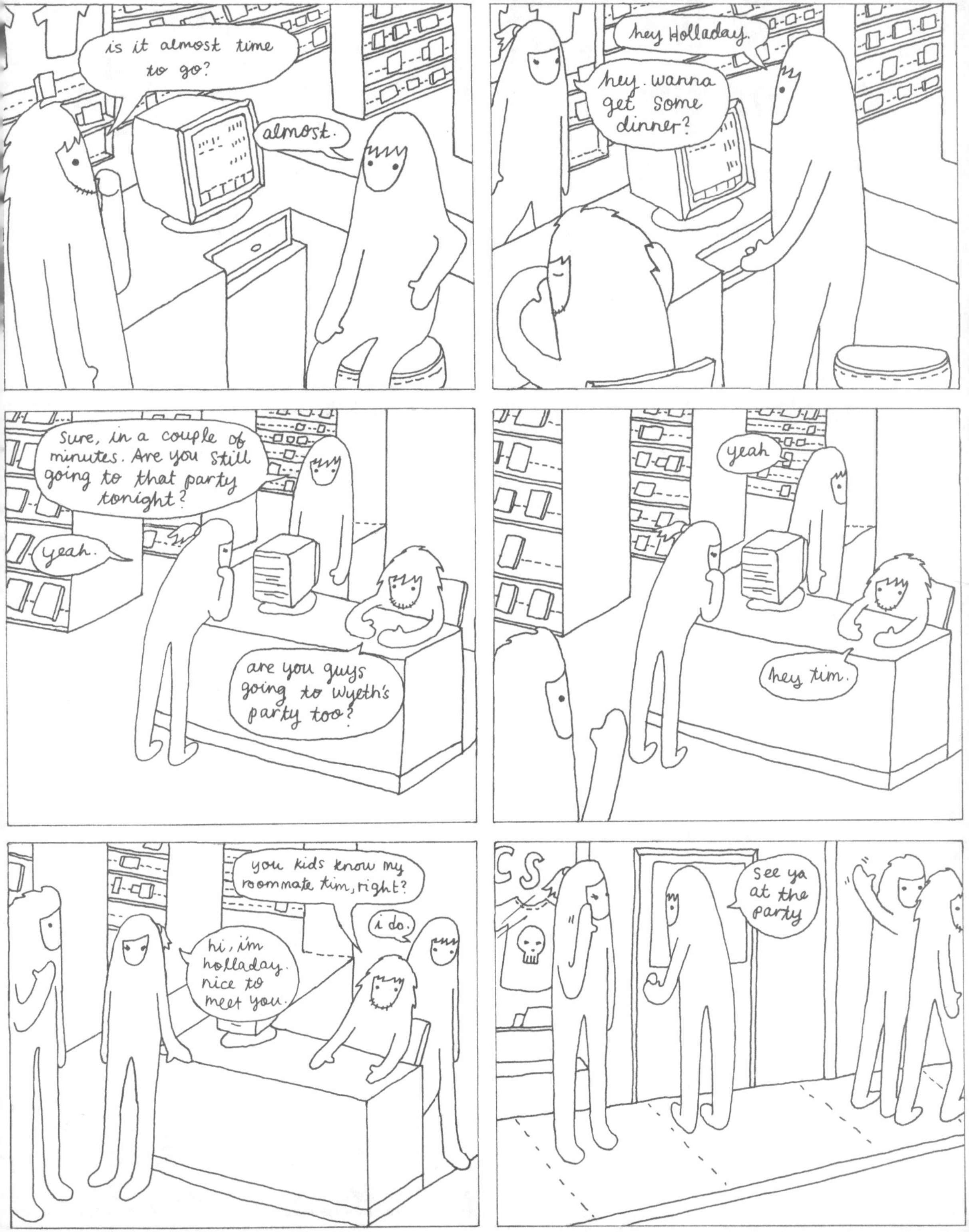
is it almost time to go?
almost.
hey Holladay.
hey. wanna get some dinner?
Sure, in a couple of minutes. Are you still going to that party tonight?
yeah.
are you guys going to Wyeth's party too?
yeah
hey tim.
you kids know my roommate tim, right?
i do.
hi, i'm holladay. nice to meet you.
CS
See ya at the party

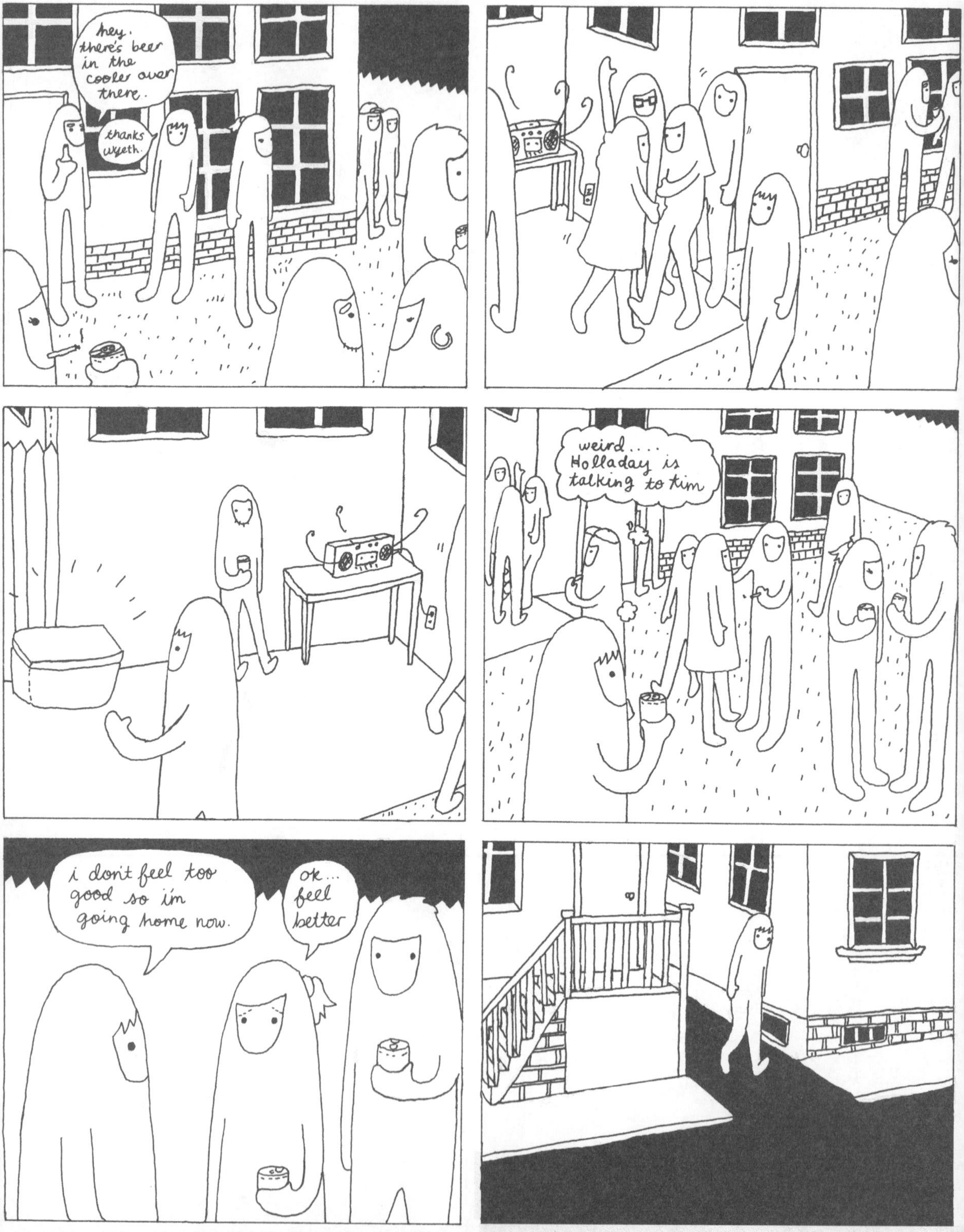
hey. there's beer in the cooler over there.
thanks wyeth.
weird.... Holladay is talking to tim
i don't feel too good so i'm going home now.
ok... feel better

RING
hello?
hey it's me
Hey...how's Australia? How was the plane?
it was long. Australia is nice, its good to see my family.
How's your internship?
it's ok, its different than i thought it would be. How are you doing?
good, just working at the comics store a lot.
Can you do me a favor?
Sure, what?
i didn't bring too much stuff with me, and all my CD's are in Providence. Can you make me an ultimate summer mix tape?
i'd love to

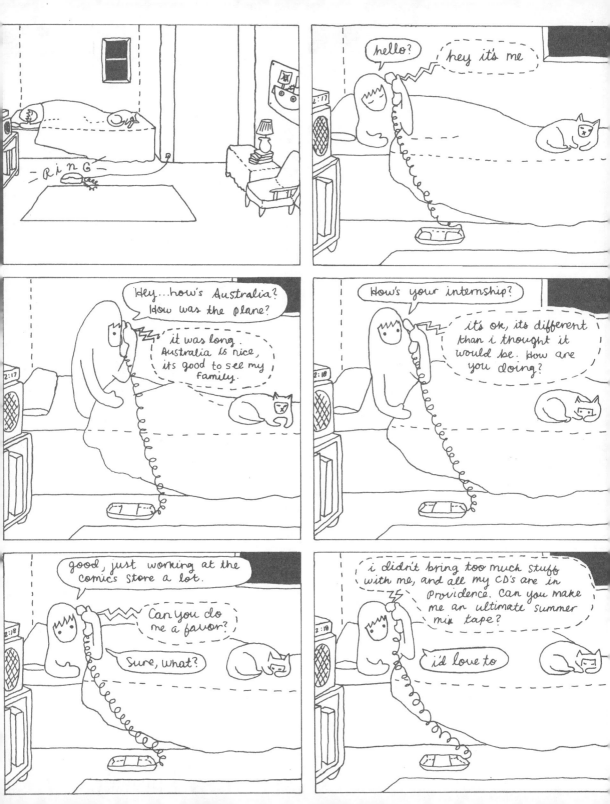

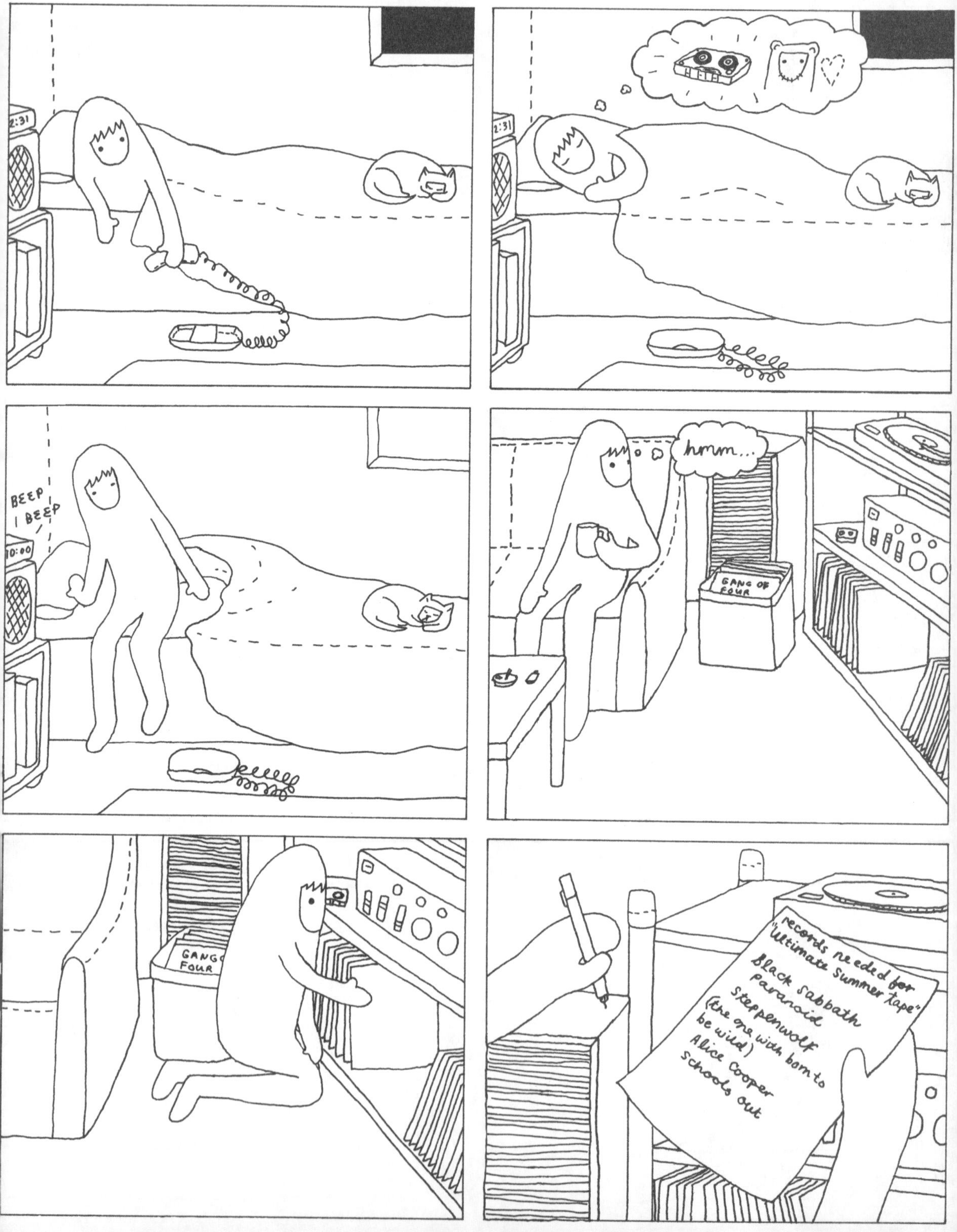
2:31
2:31
BEEP BEEP
10:00
hmm...
GANG OF FOUR
records needed for "Ultimate Summer tape"
Black Sabbath
Paranoid
Steppenwolf
(the one with born to be wild)
Alice Cooper
Schools out

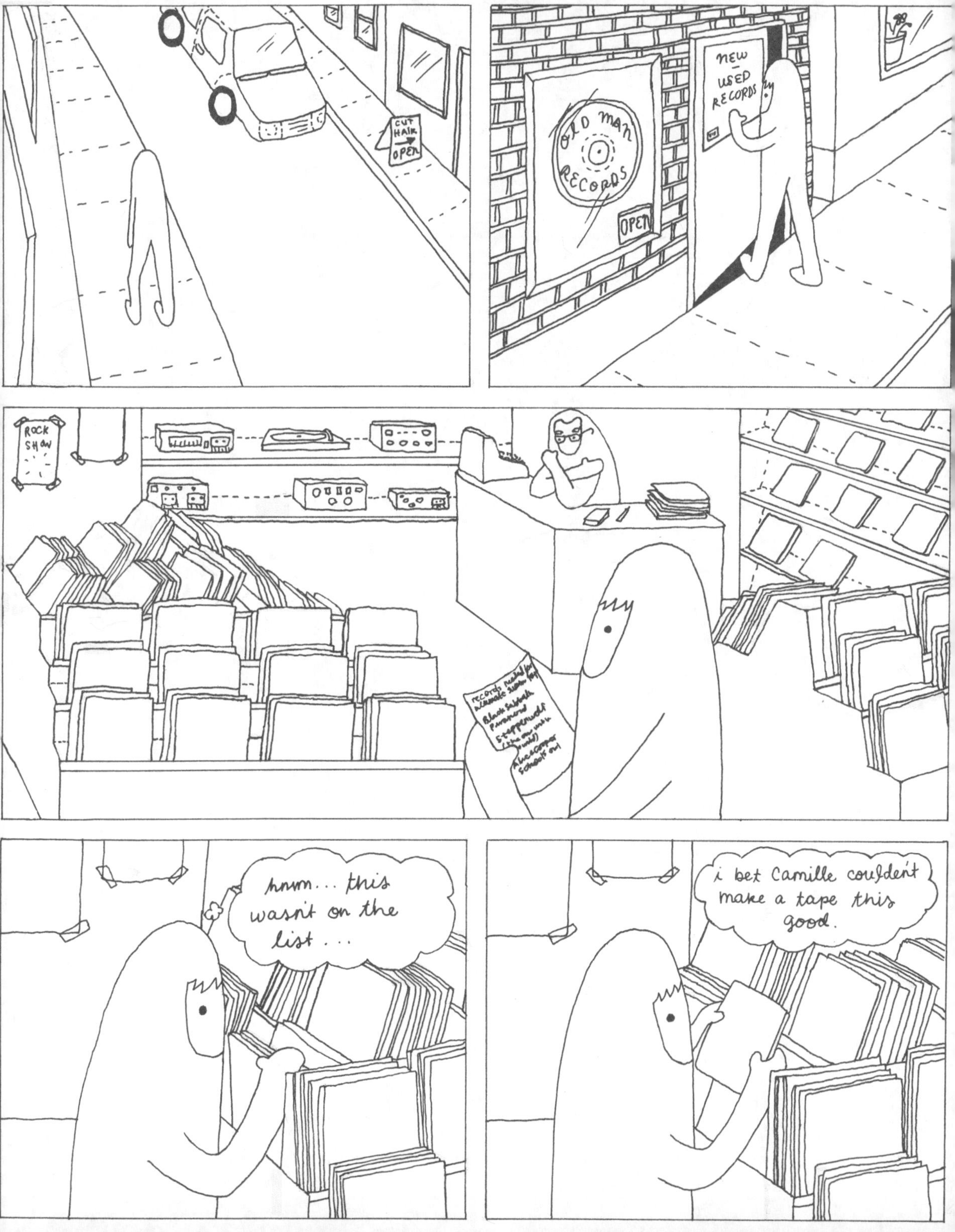
CUT HAIR
OPEN
OLD MAN RECORDS
OPEN
NEW
-
USED RECORDS
ROCK SHOW
records needed for
Black Sabbath
Paranoid
Steppenwolf
Alice Cooper
Schools out
hmm... this wasn't on the list...
i bet Camille couldn't make a tape this good.

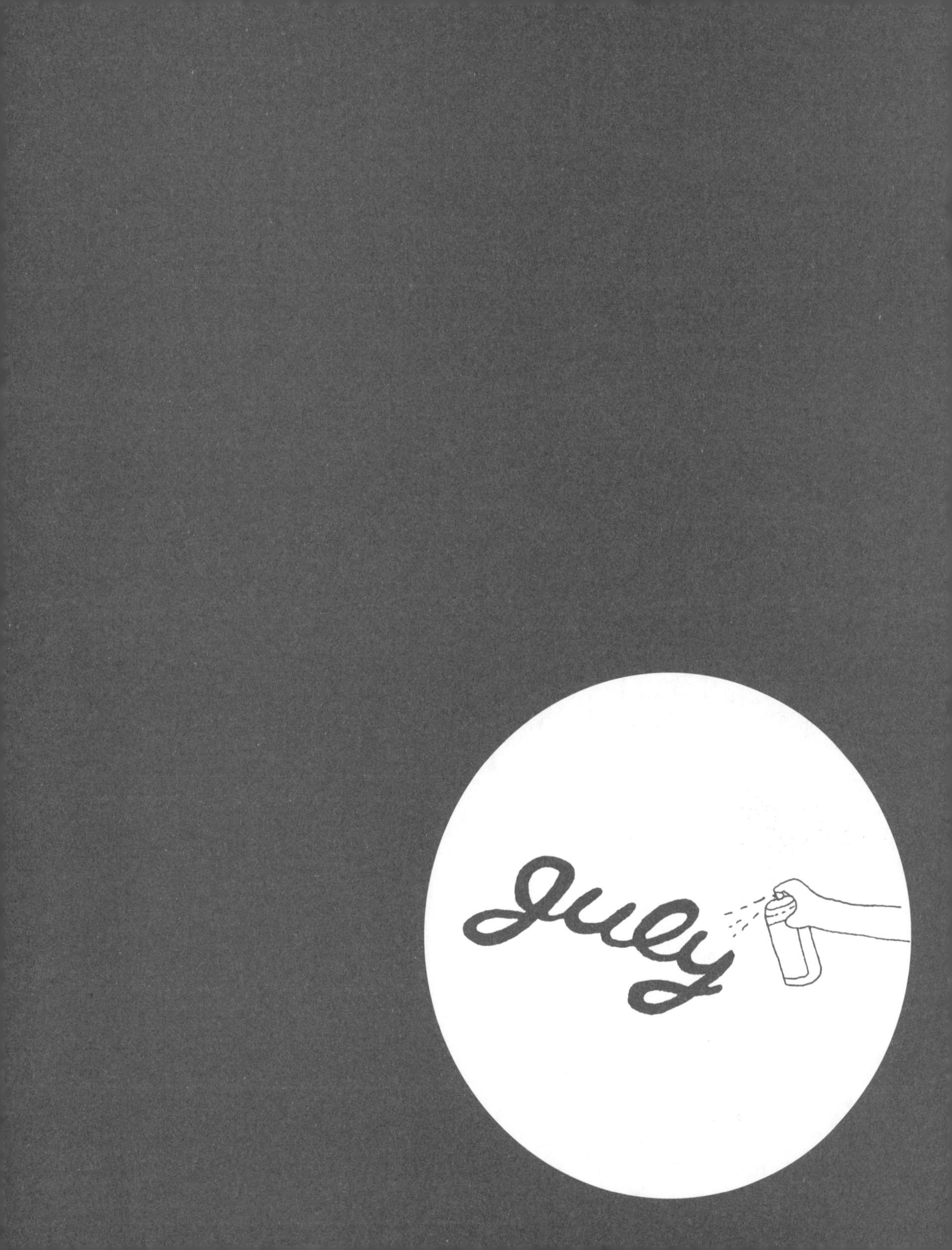
July

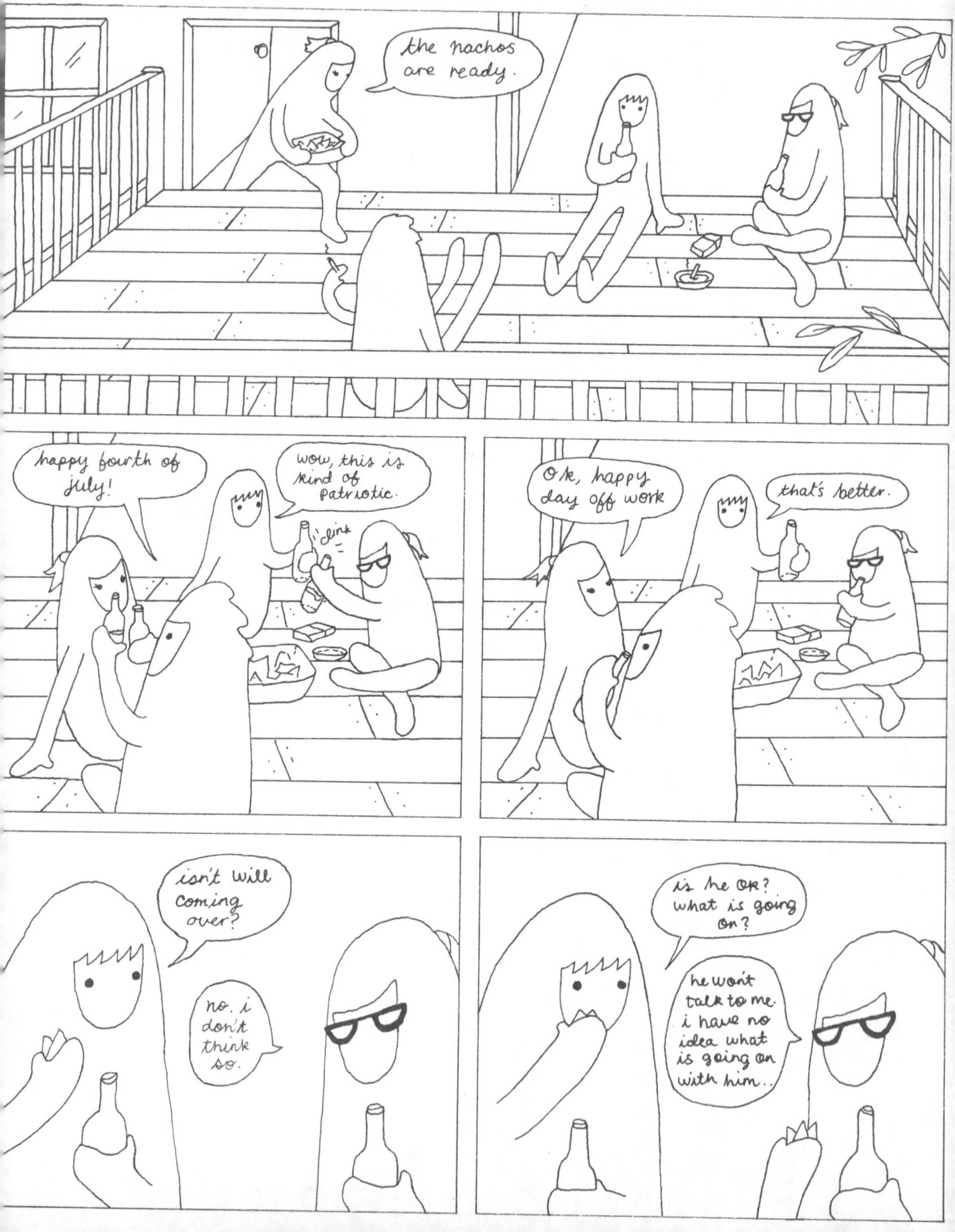

the nachos are ready.
happy fourth of july!
wow, this is kind of patriotic.
clink
Ok, happy day off work
that's better.
isn't Will coming over?
no. i don't think so.
is he OK? what is going on?
he won't talk to me. i have no idea what is going on with him..

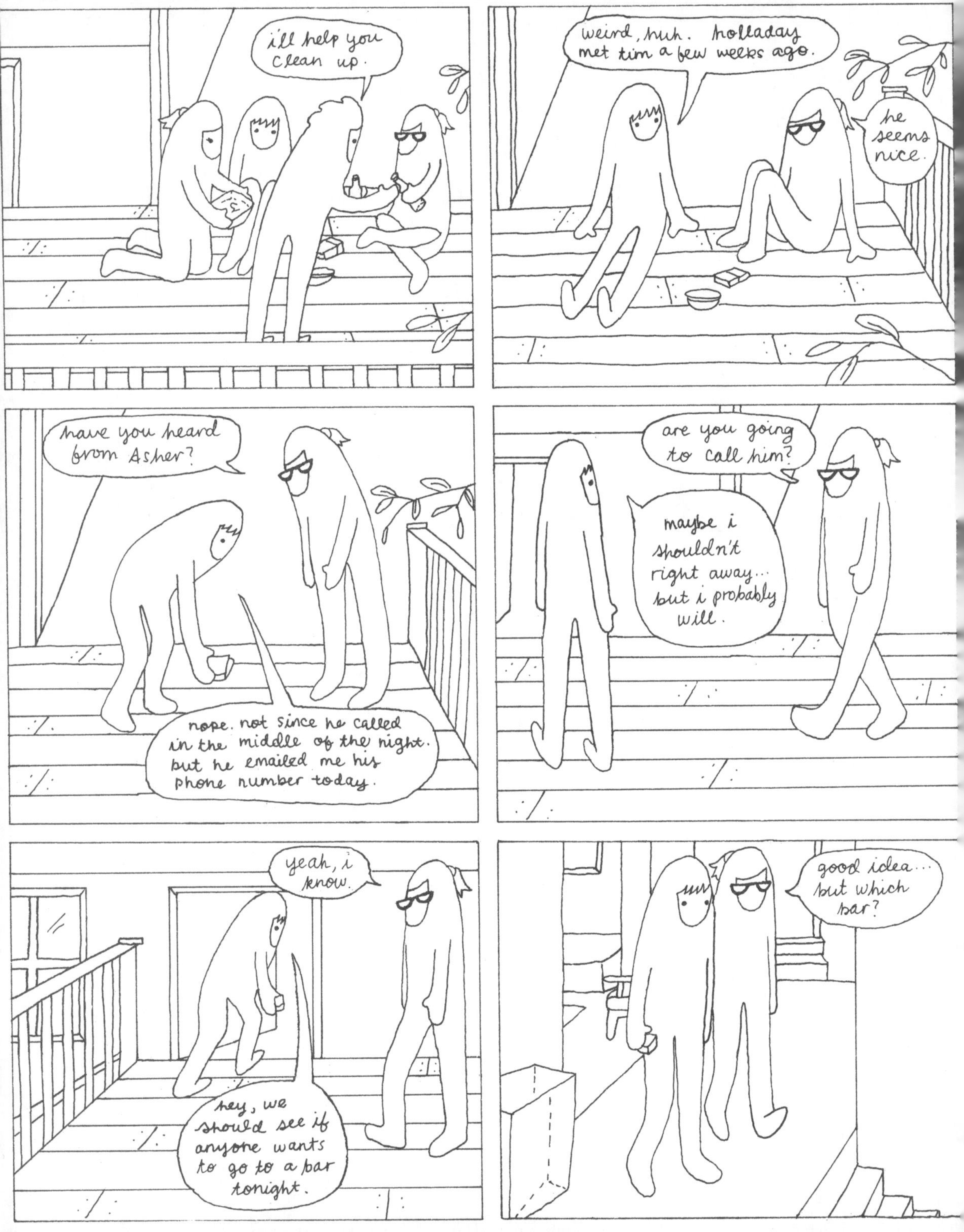

i'll help you clean up.
weird, huh. holladay met tim a few weeks ago.
he seems nice.
have you heard from Asher?
nope. not since he called in the middle of the night. but he emailed me his phone number today.
are you going to call him?
maybe i shouldn't right away... but i probably will.
yeah, i know.
hey, we should see if anyone wants to go to a bar tonight.
good idea... but which bar?

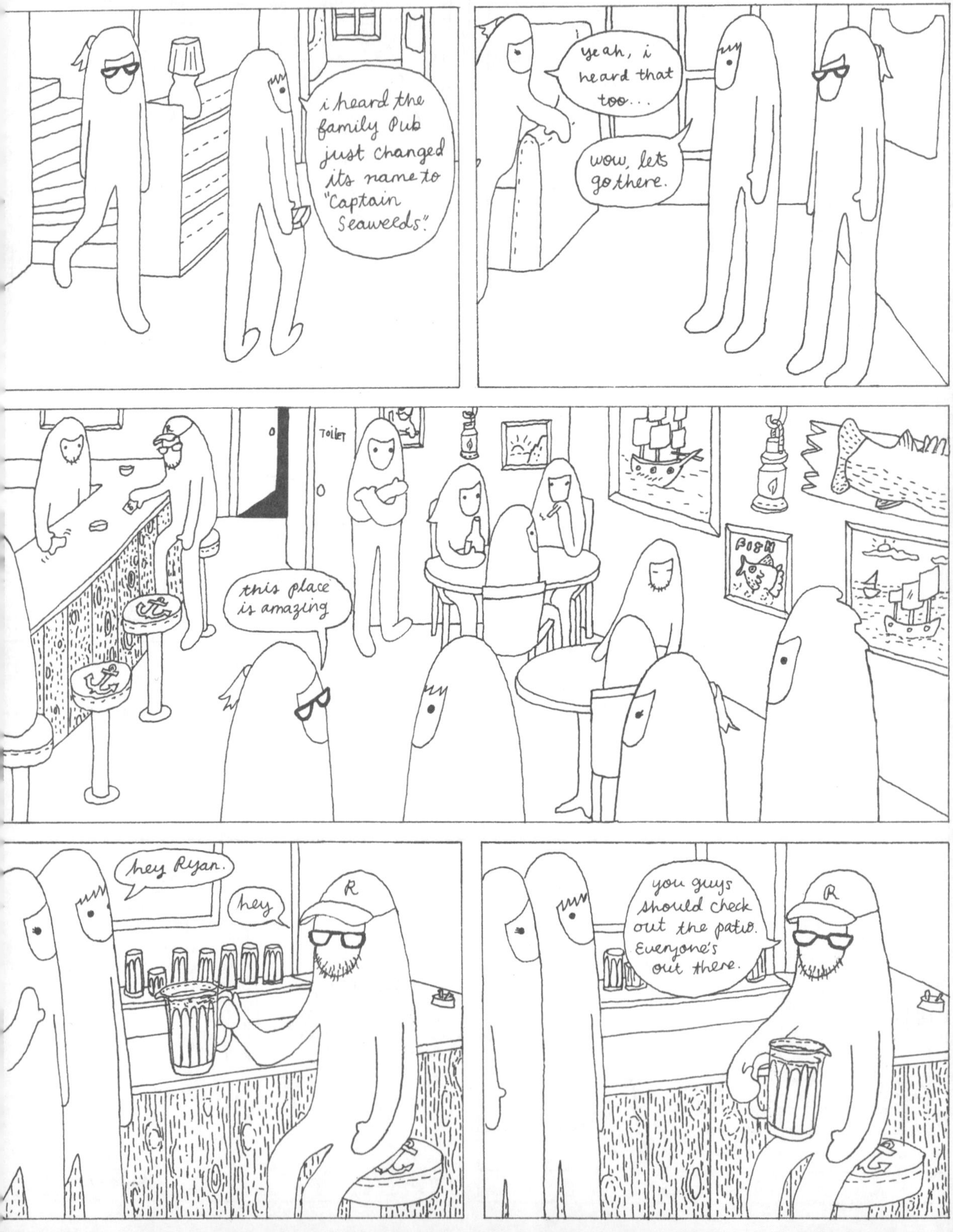
i heard the family Pub just changed its name to "Captain Seaweeds".
yeah, i heard that too...
wow, lets go there.
TOILET
FISH
this place is amazing
hey Ryan.
hey
R
R
you guys should check out the patio. Everyone's out there.

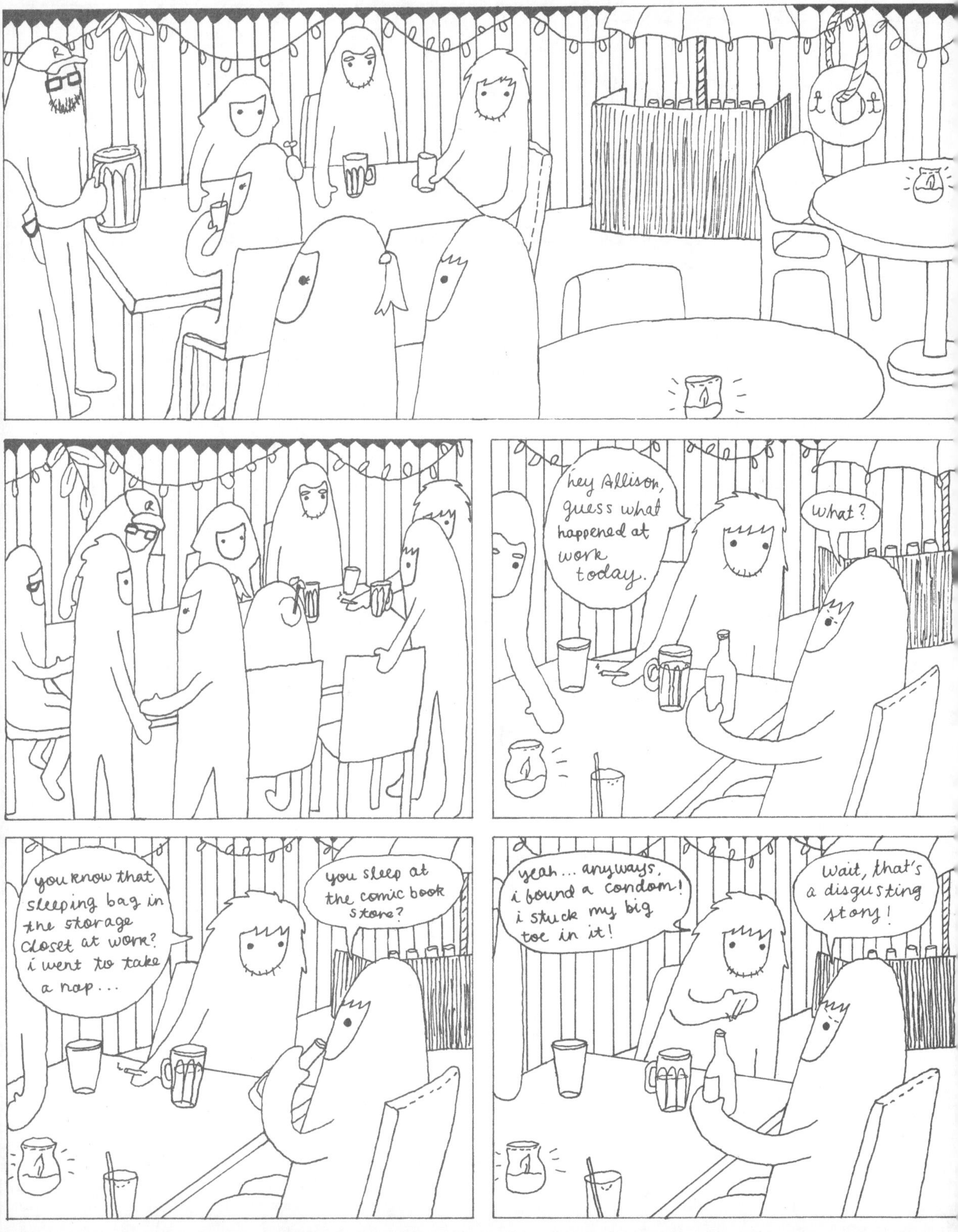
hey Allison, guess what happened at work today.
What?
you know that sleeping bag in the storage closet at work? i went to take a nap...
you sleep at the comic book store?
yeah... anyways, i found a condom! i stuck my big toe in it!
Wait, that's a disgusting story!

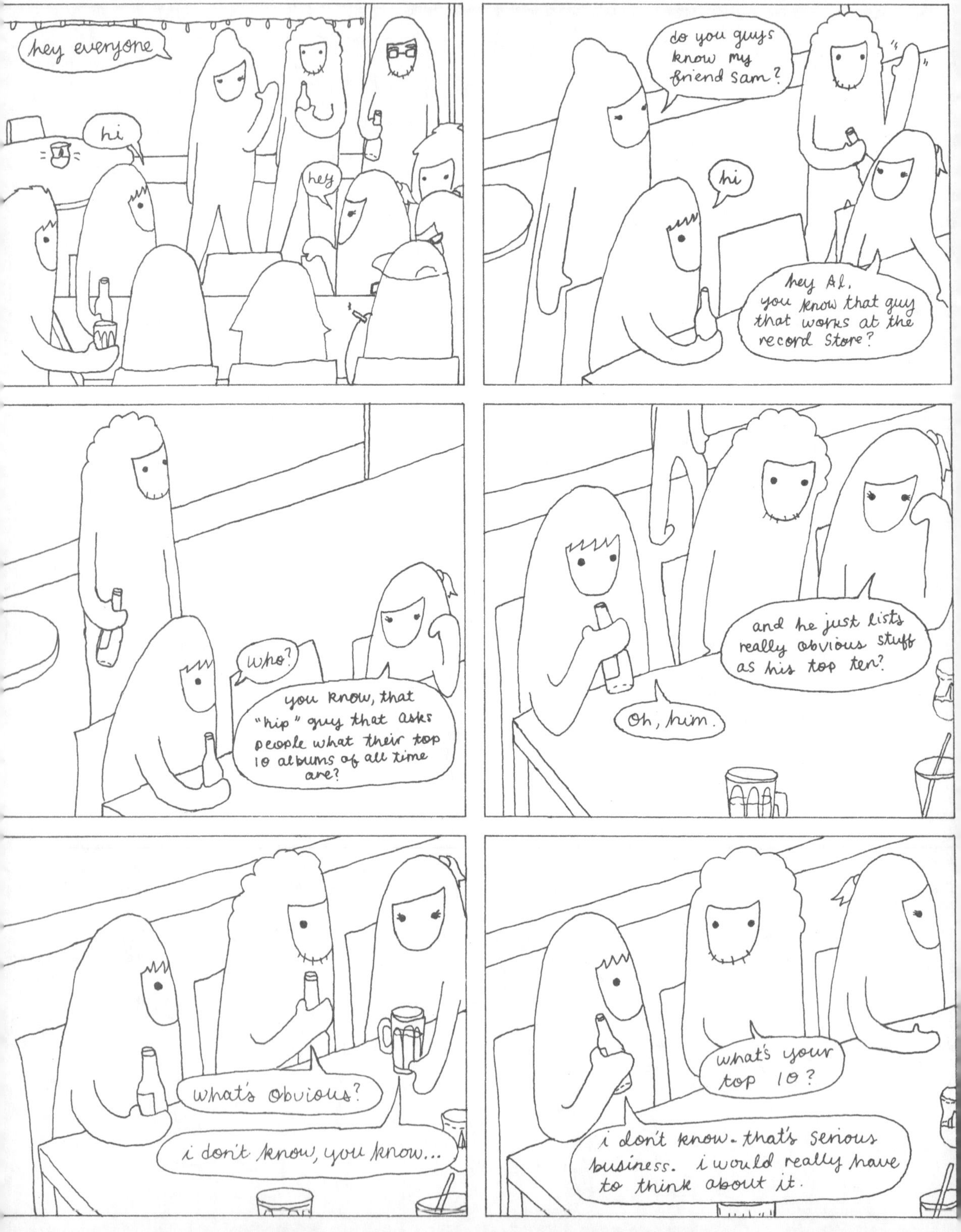
hey everyone
hi
hey
do you guys know my friend sam?
hi
hey Al, you know that guy that works at the record store?
who?
you know, that "hip" guy that asks people what their top 10 albums of all time are?
and he just lists really obvious stuff as his top ten?
Oh, him.
what's obvious?
i don't know, you know...
what's your top 10?
i don't know. that's serious business. i would really have to think about it.

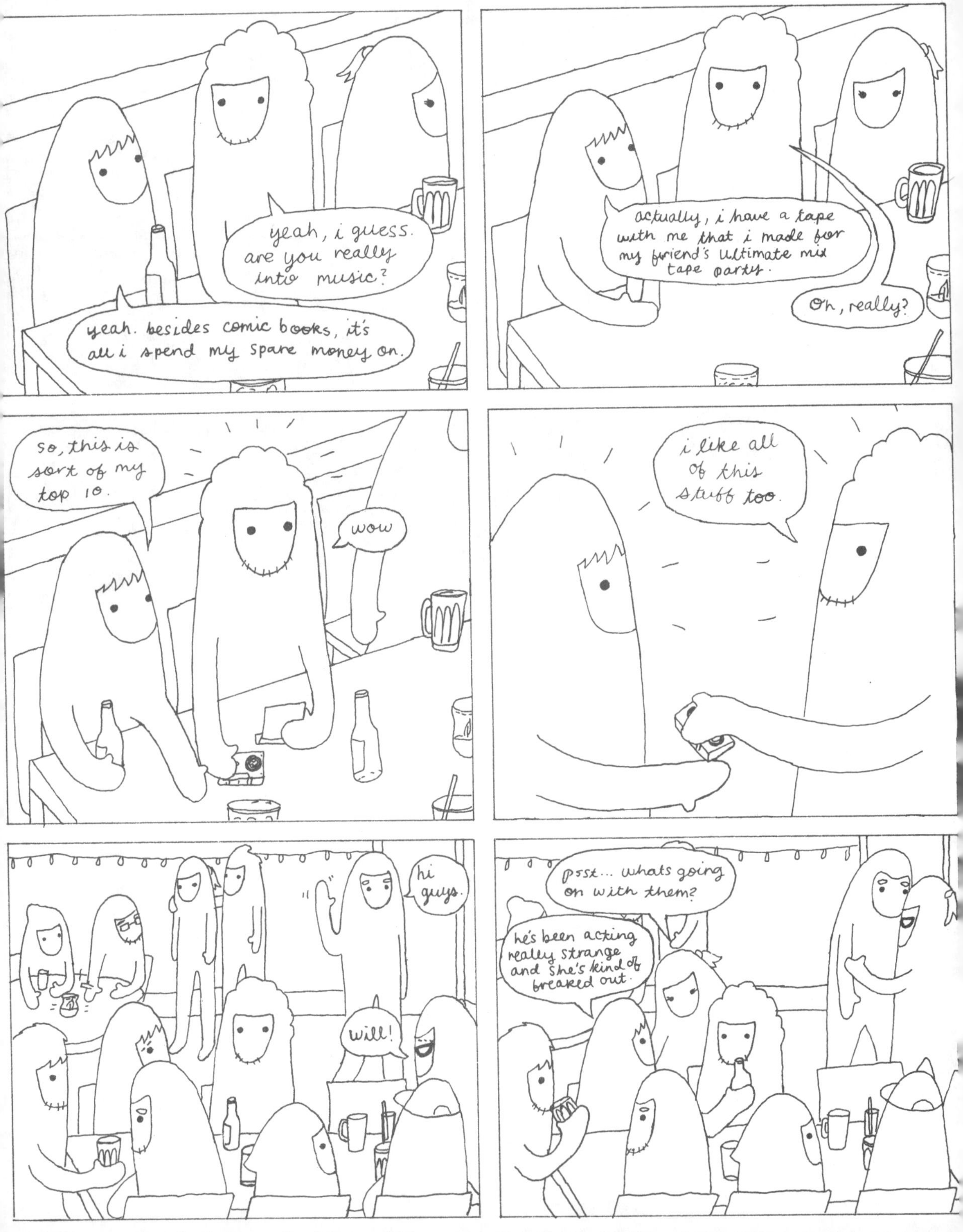
yeah, i guess. are you really into music?
yeah. besides comic books, it's all i spend my spare money on.
actually, i have a tape with me that i made for my friend's Ultimate mix tape party.
Oh, really?
so, this is sort of my top 10.
wow
i like all of this stuff too.
hi guys.
will!
psst... whats going on with them?
he's been acting realey strange and she's kind of freaked out.

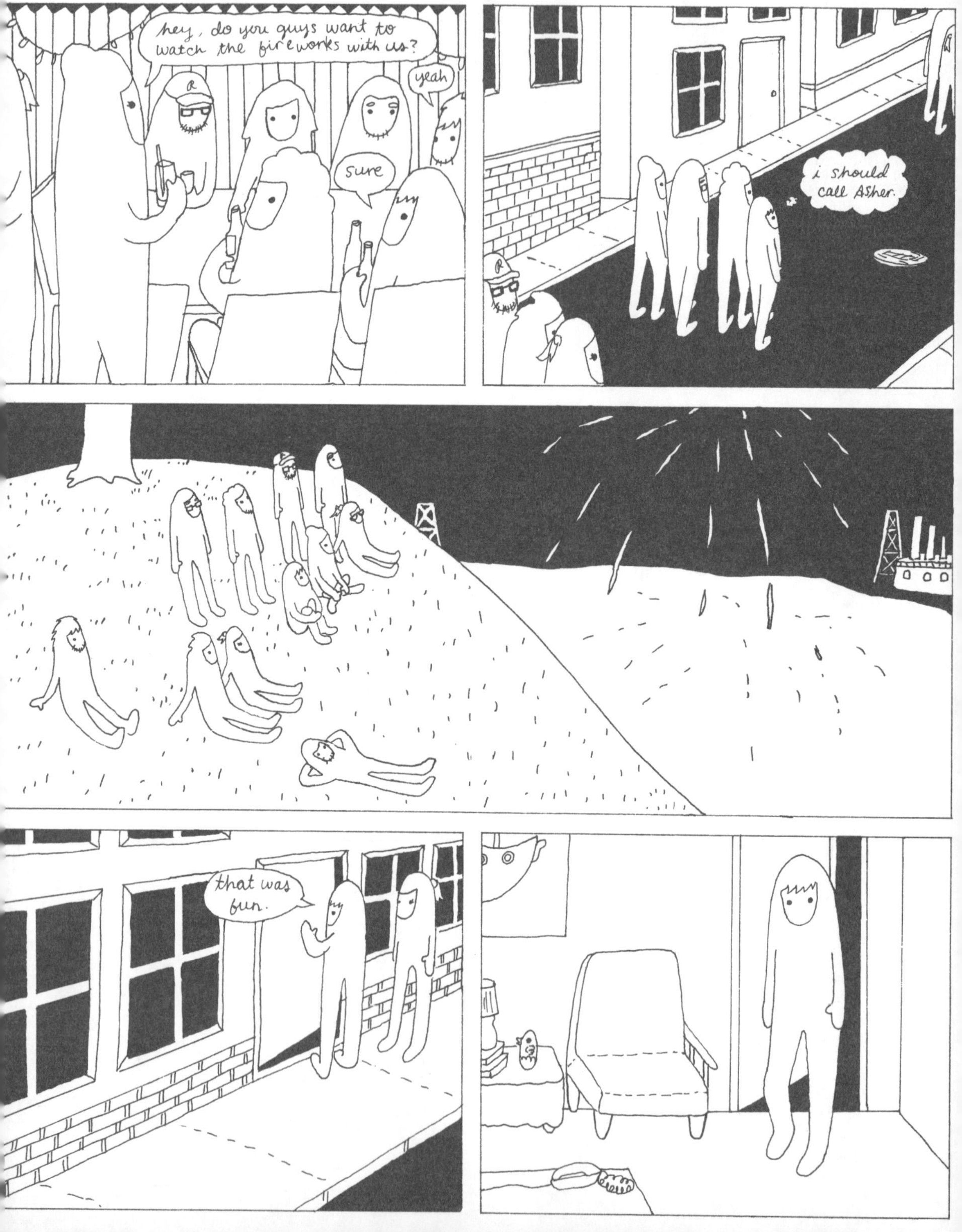
hey, do you guys want to watch the fireworks with us?
yeah
sure
i should call Asher.
that was fun.

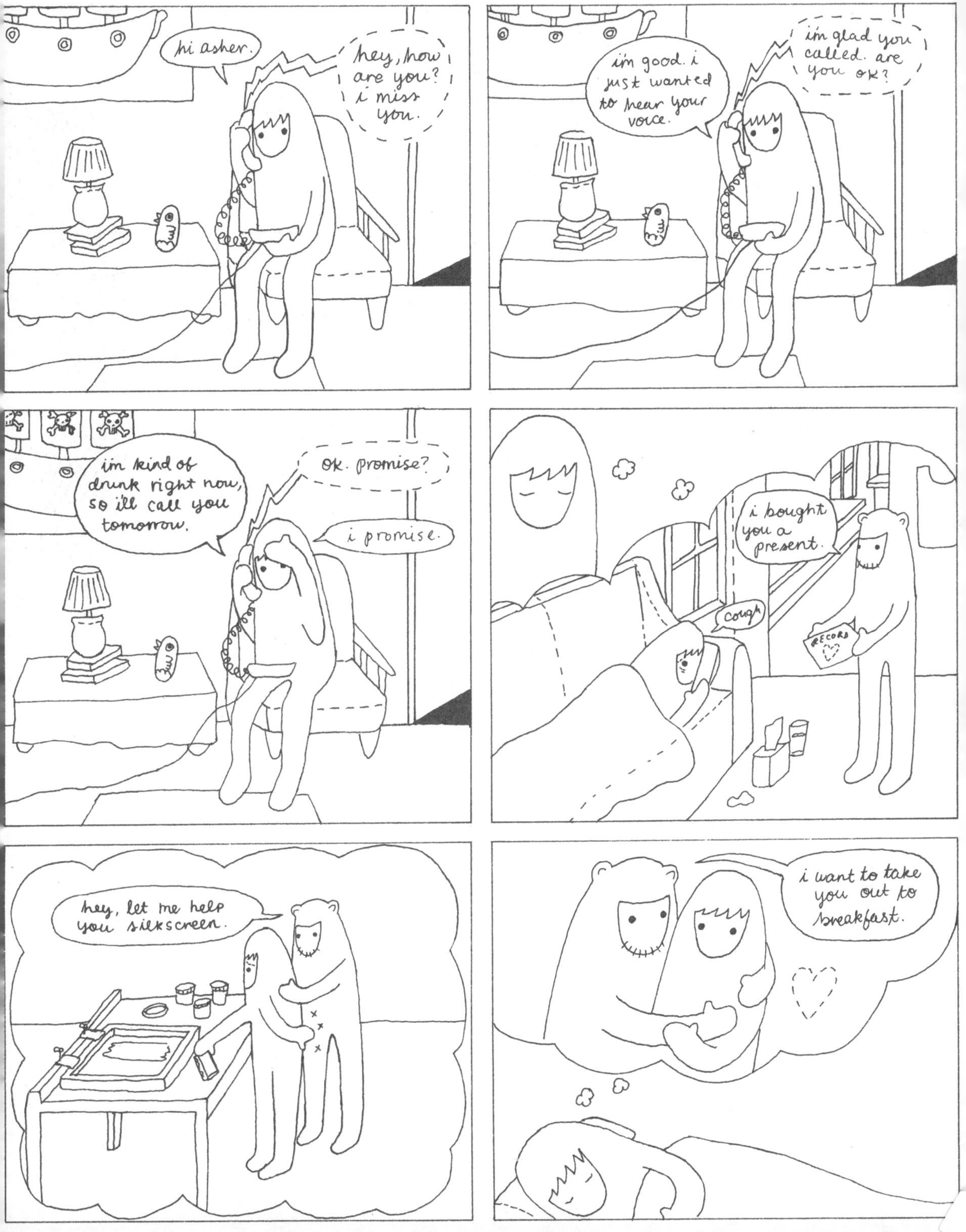

hi asher.
hey, how are you? i miss you.
im good. i just wanted to hear your voice.
im glad you called. are you ok?
im kind of drunk right now, so ill call you tomorrow.
ok. promise?
i promise.
i bought you a present.
cough
RECORD
hey, let me help you silkscreen.
i want to take you out to breakfast.

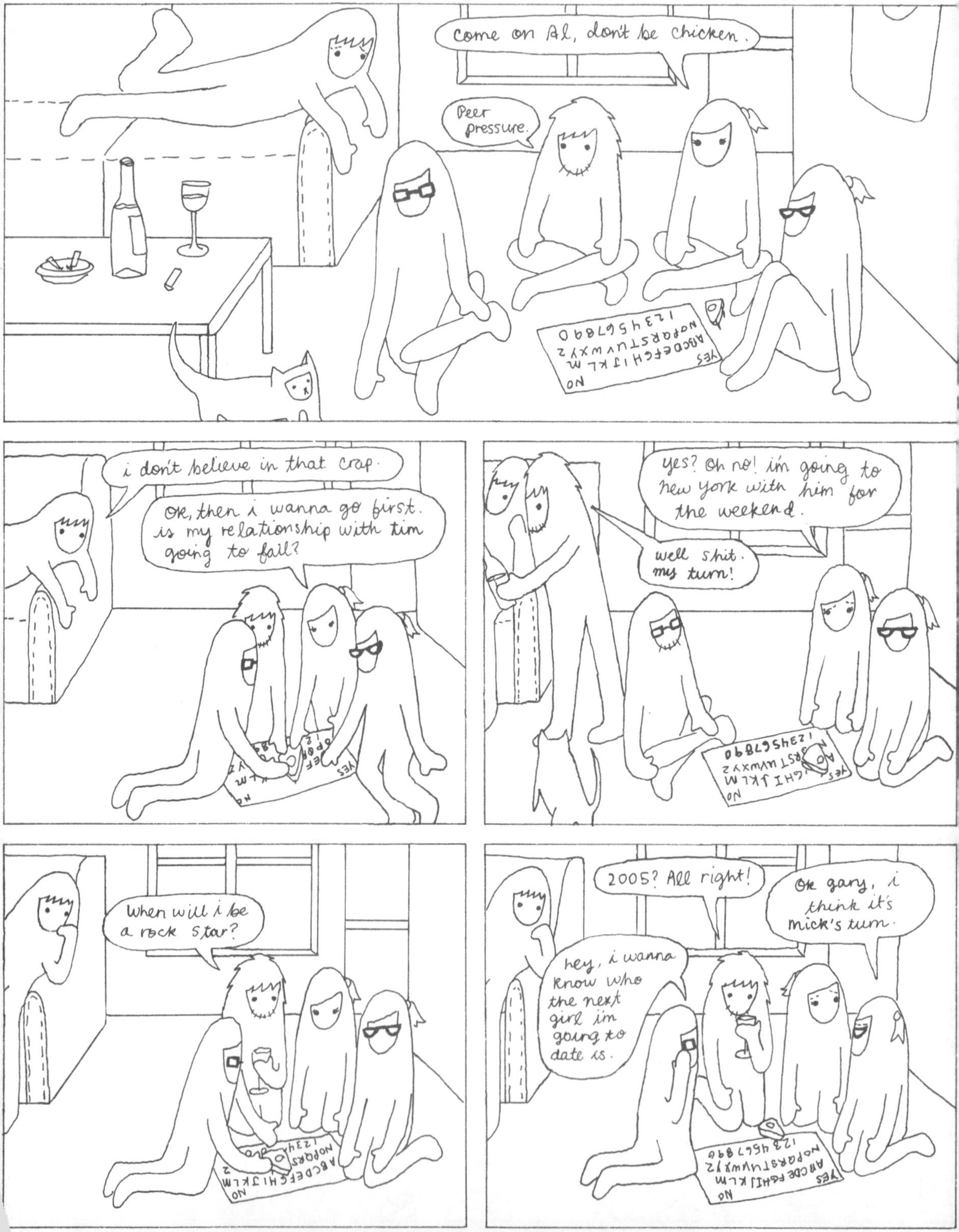
Come on Al, don't be chicken.
Peer pressure.
i don't believe in that crap.
Ok, then i wanna go first. is my relationship with tim going to fail?
Yes? Oh no! i'm going to New York with him for the weekend.
well shit. my turn!
When will i be a rock star?
2005? All right!
Ok gary, i think it's mick's turn.
hey, i wanna know who the next girl im going to date is.

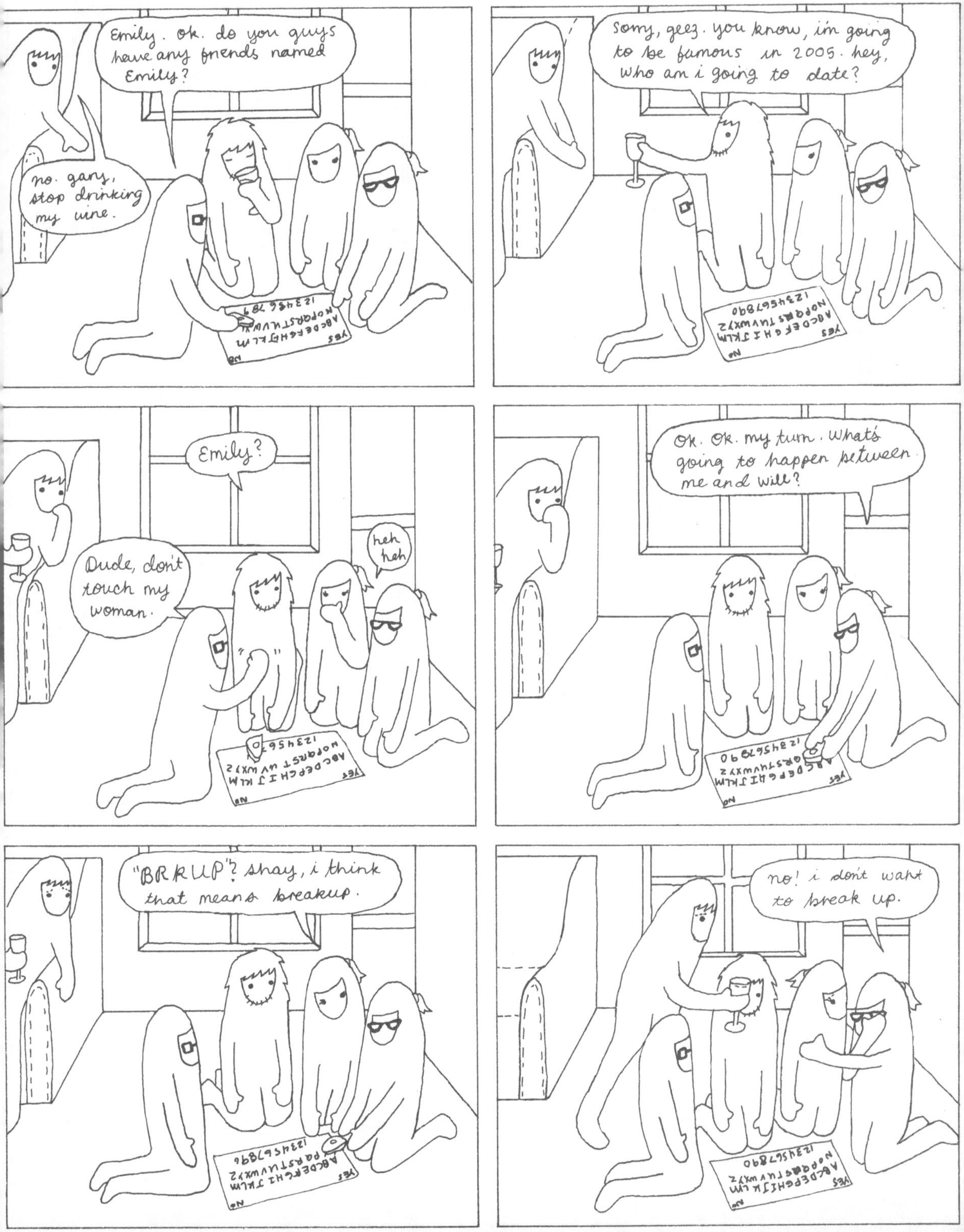
Emily. Ok. do you guys have any friends named Emily?
no. gary, stop drinking my wine.
Sorry, geez. you know, i'm going to be famous in 2005. hey, Who am i going to date?
Emily?
Dude, don't touch my woman.
heh heh
Ok. Ok. my turn. What's going to happen between me and Will?
"BRKUP"? shay, i think that means breakup.
no! i don't want to break up.

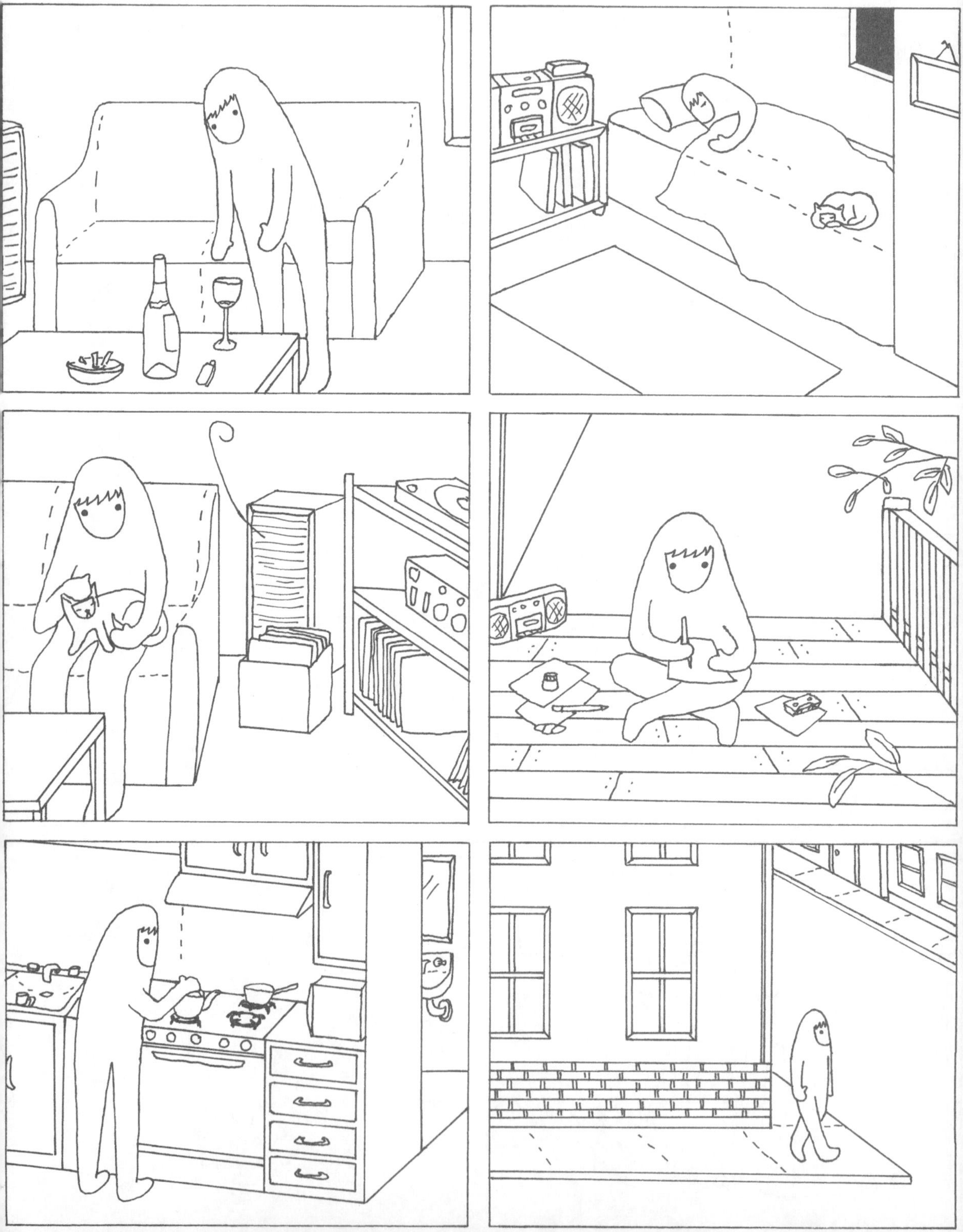

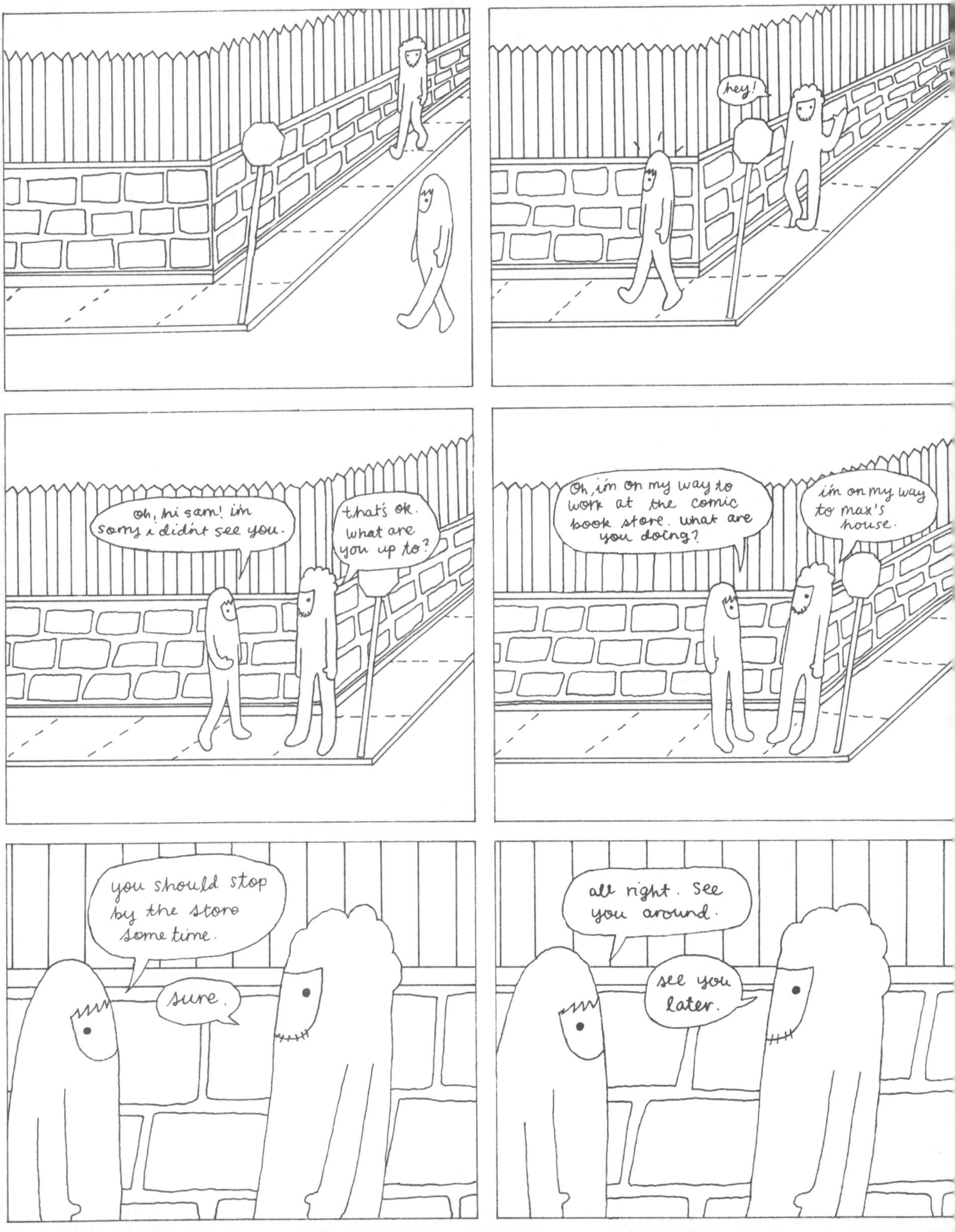
hey!
oh, hi sam! i'm sorry i didn't see you.
that's ok. what are you up to?
oh, i'm on my way to work at the comic book store. what are you doing?
i'm on my way to max's house.
you should stop by the store some time.
sure.
all right. see you around.
see you later.

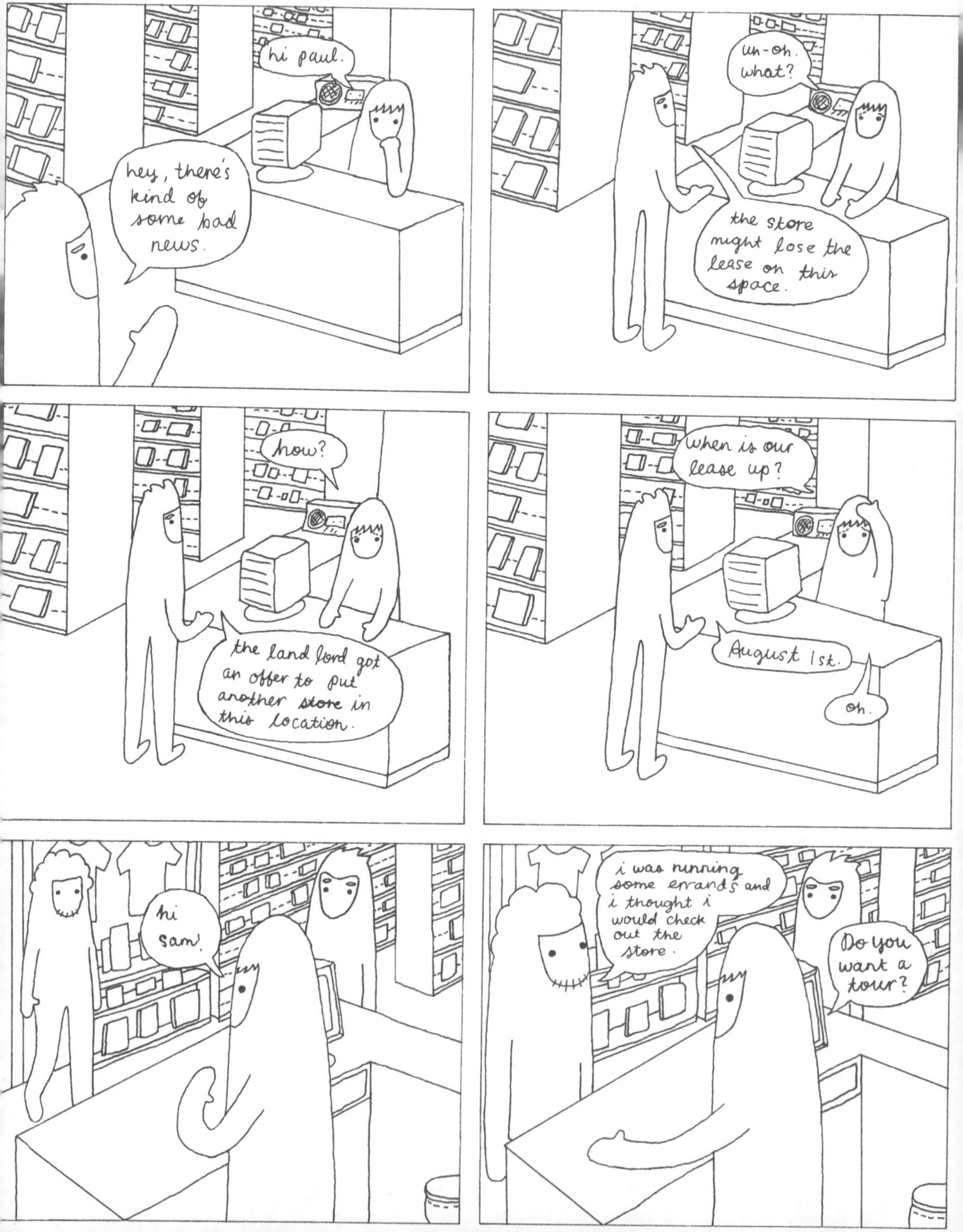
hi paul.
hey, there's kind of some bad news.
uh-oh. what?
the store might lose the lease on this space.
how?
the land lord got an offer to put another store in this location.
when is our lease up?
August 1st.
oh.
hi sam!
i was running some errands and i thought i would check out the store.
Do you want a tour?

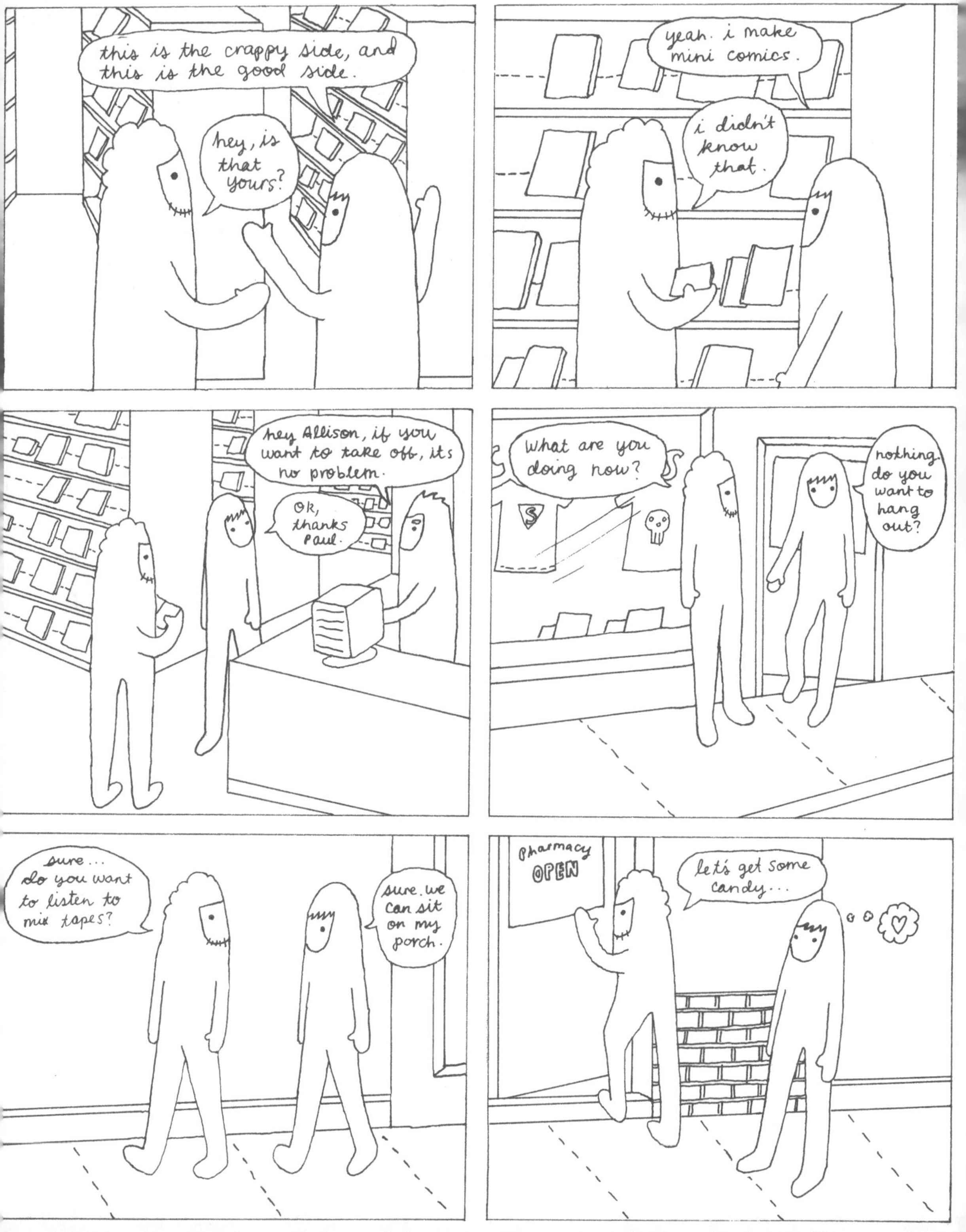
this is the crappy side, and this is the good side.
hey, is that yours?
yeah. i make mini comics.
i didn't know that.
hey Allison, if you want to take off, it's no problem.
Ok, thanks Paul.
What are you doing now?
nothing. do you want to hang out?
sure... do you want to listen to mix tapes?
sure. we can sit on my porch.
Pharmacy OPEN
let's get some candy...

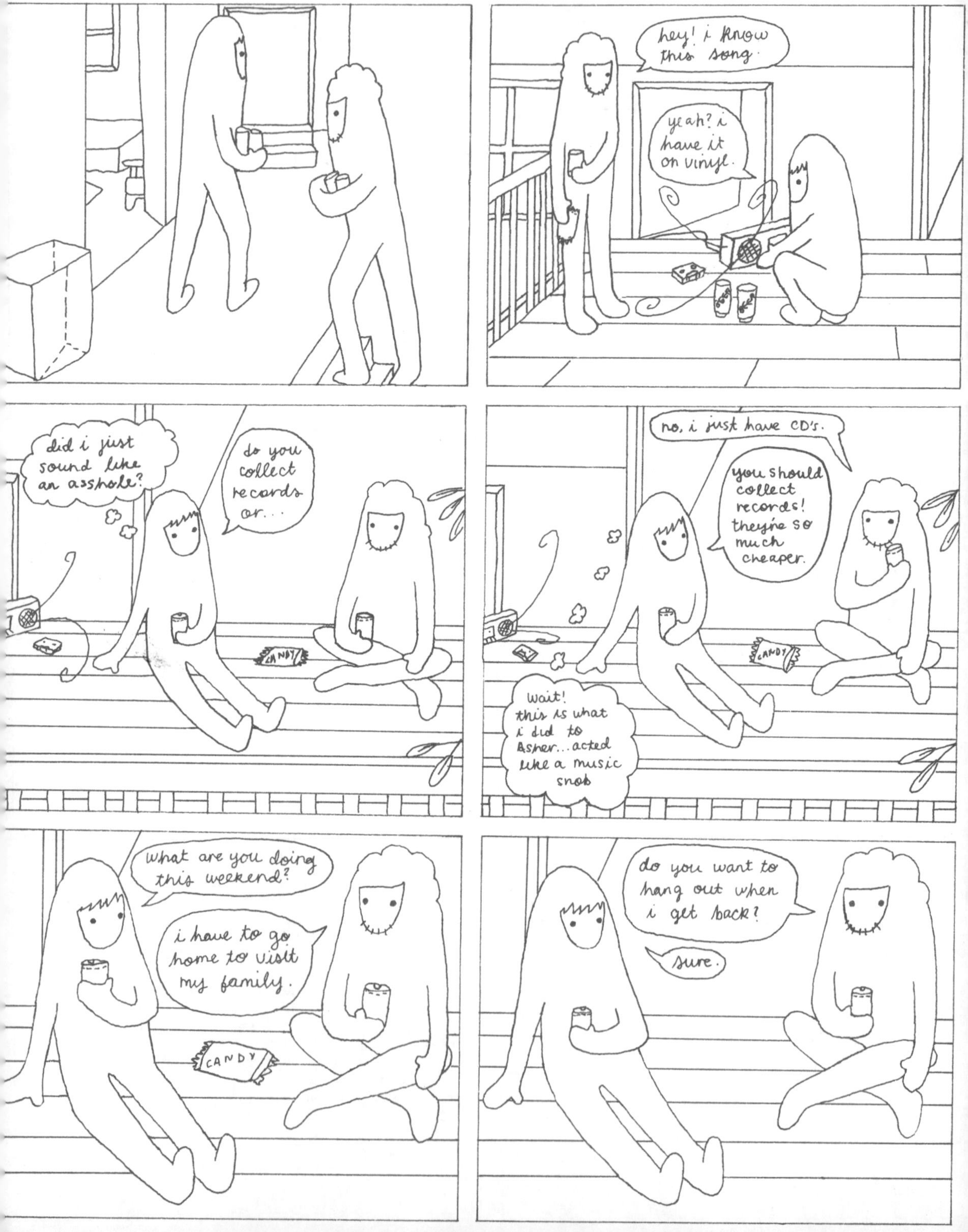

hey! i know this song.
yeah? i have it on vinyl.
did i just sound like an asshole?
do you collect records or...
no, i just have CD's.
you should collect records! they're so much cheaper.
CANDY
wait! this is what i did to Asher... acted like a music snob
what are you doing this weekend?
i have to go home to visit my family.
CANDY
do you want to hang out when i get back?
sure.

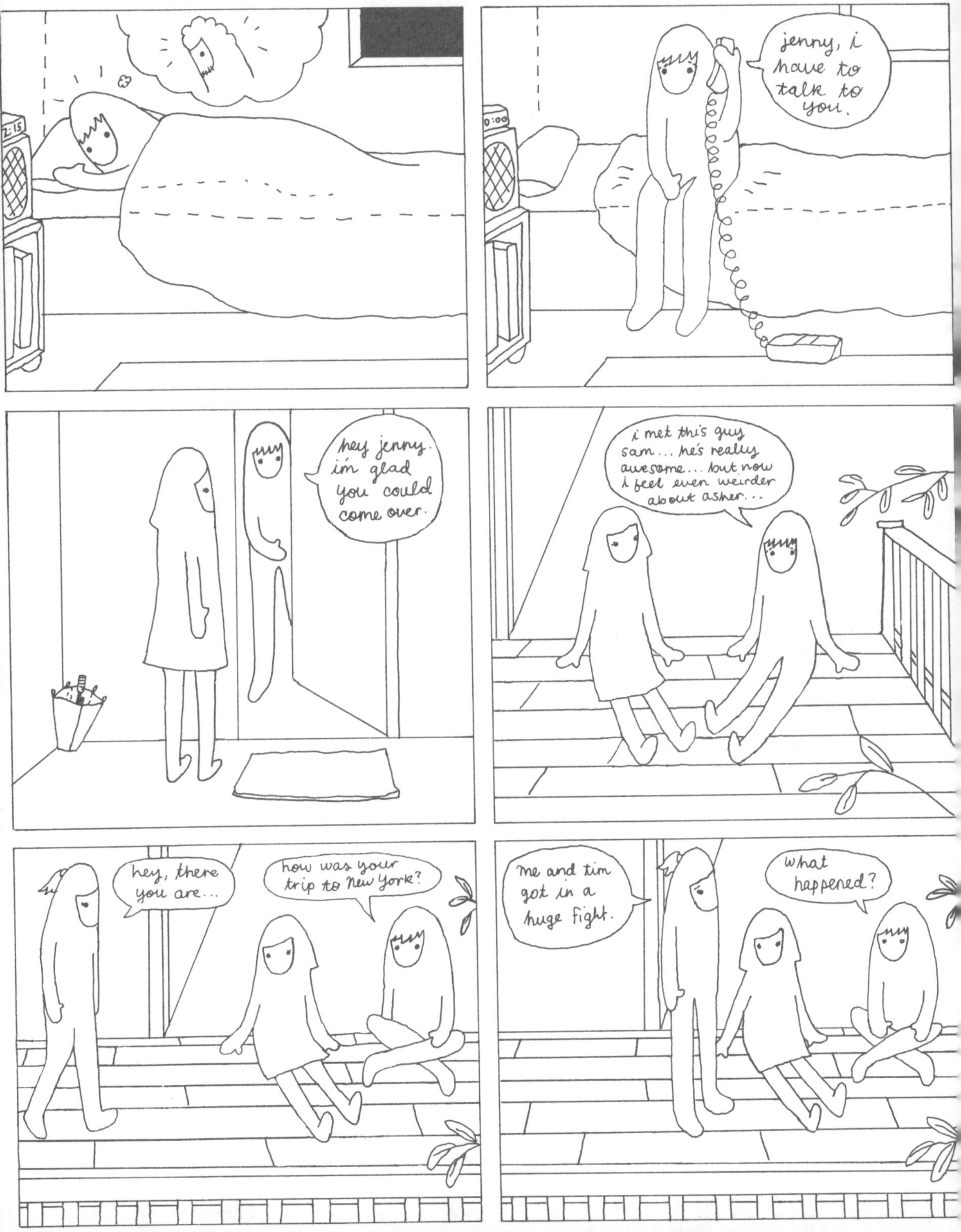
2:15
jenny, i have to talk to you.
hey jenny. i'm glad you could come over.
i met this guy sam... he's really awesome... but now i feel even weirder about asher...
hey, there you are...
how was your trip to New York?
me and tim got in a huge fight.
what happened?

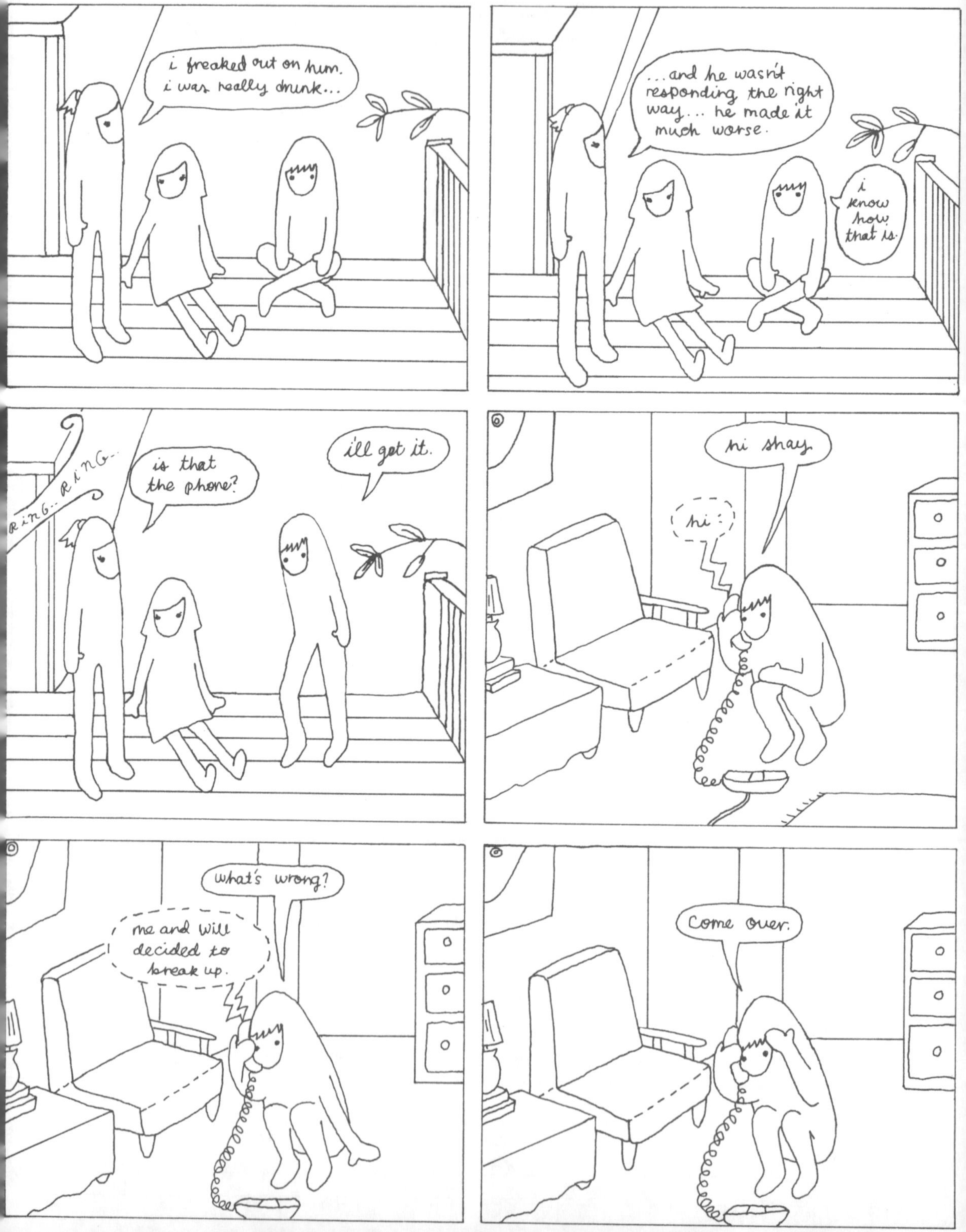
i freaked out on him. i was really drunk...
...and he wasn't responding the right way... he made it much worse.
i know how that is.
RING... RING...
is that the phone?
i'll get it.
hi shay.
hi
what's wrong?
me and will decided to break up.
Come over.

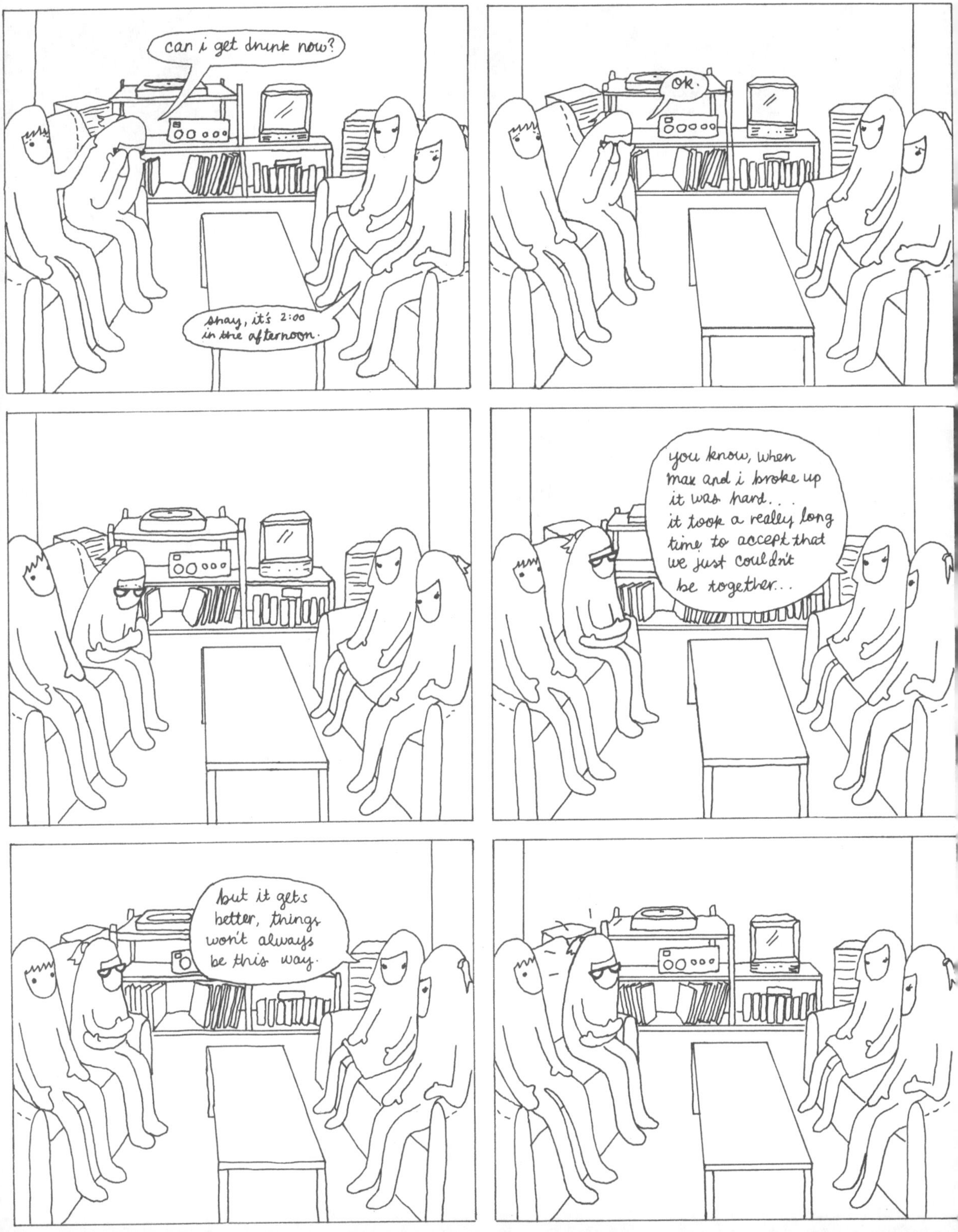
can i get drunk now?
shay, it's 2:00 in the afternoon.
ok.
you know, when max and i broke up it was hard... it took a really long time to accept that we just couldn't be together...
but it gets better, things won't always be this way.

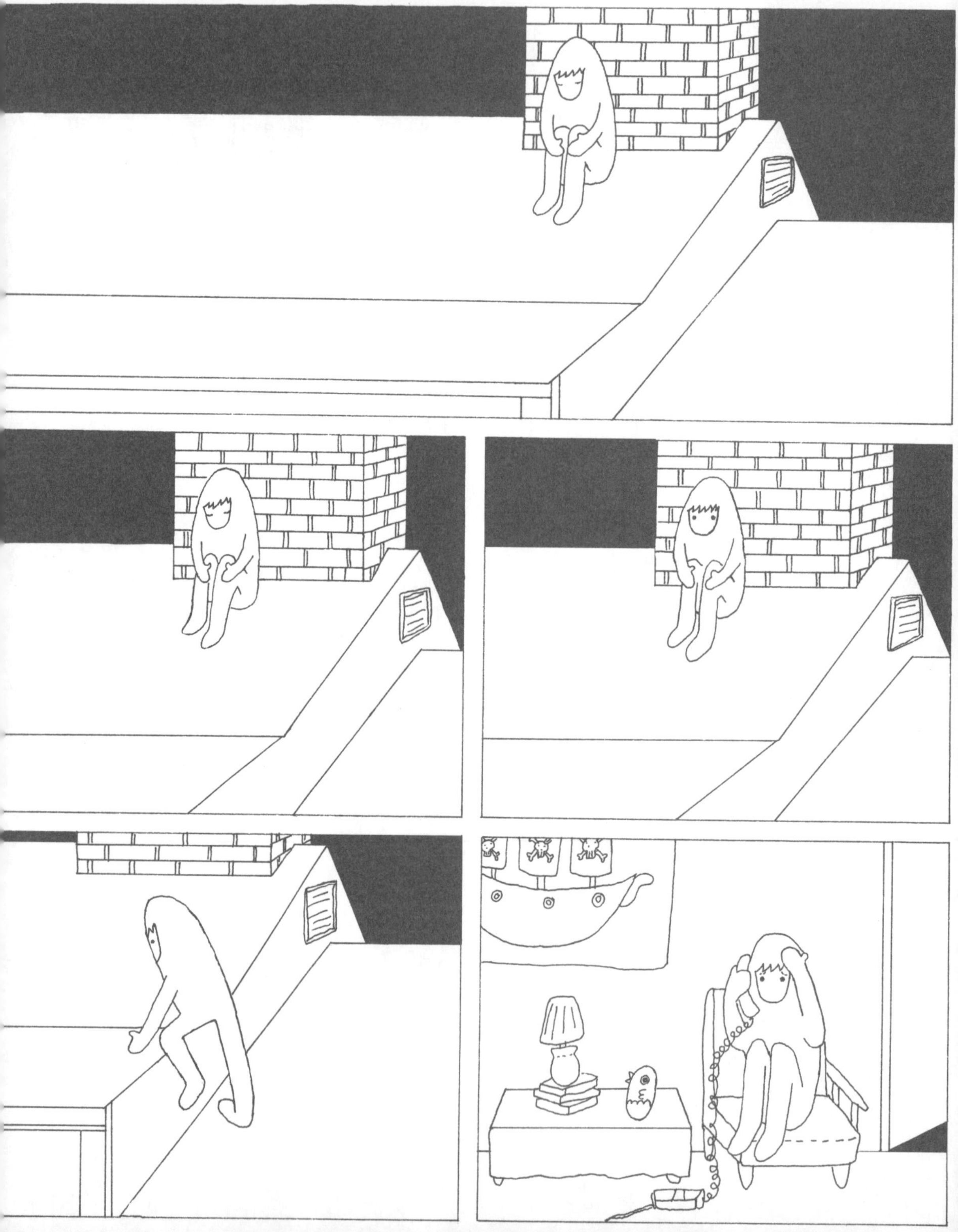

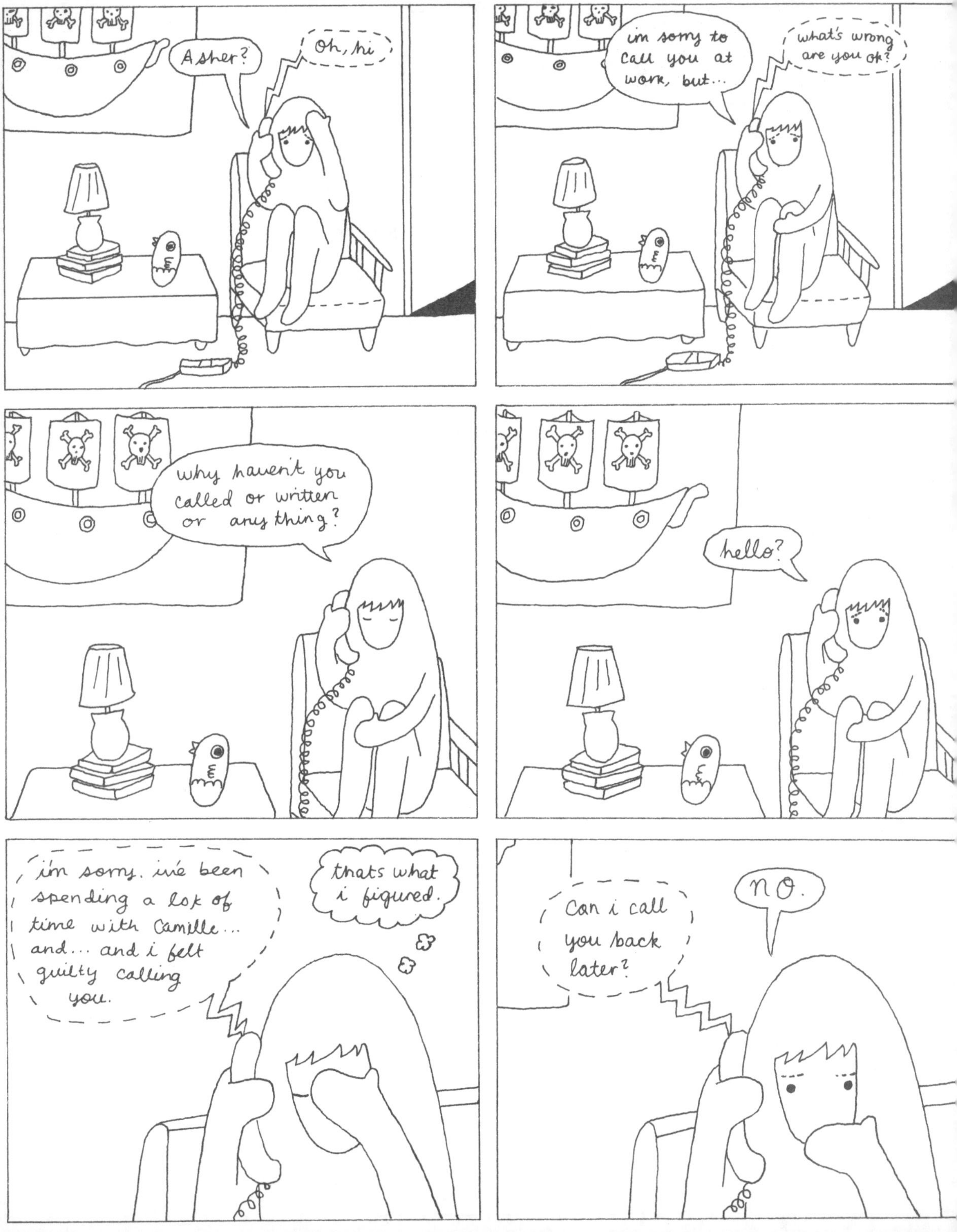
Asher?
Oh, hi
im sorry to call you at work, but...
what's wrong are you ok?
why haven't you called or written or anything?
hello?
im sorry. ive been spending a lot of time with Camille... and... and i felt guilty calling you.
thats what i figured.
Can i call you back later?
NO.

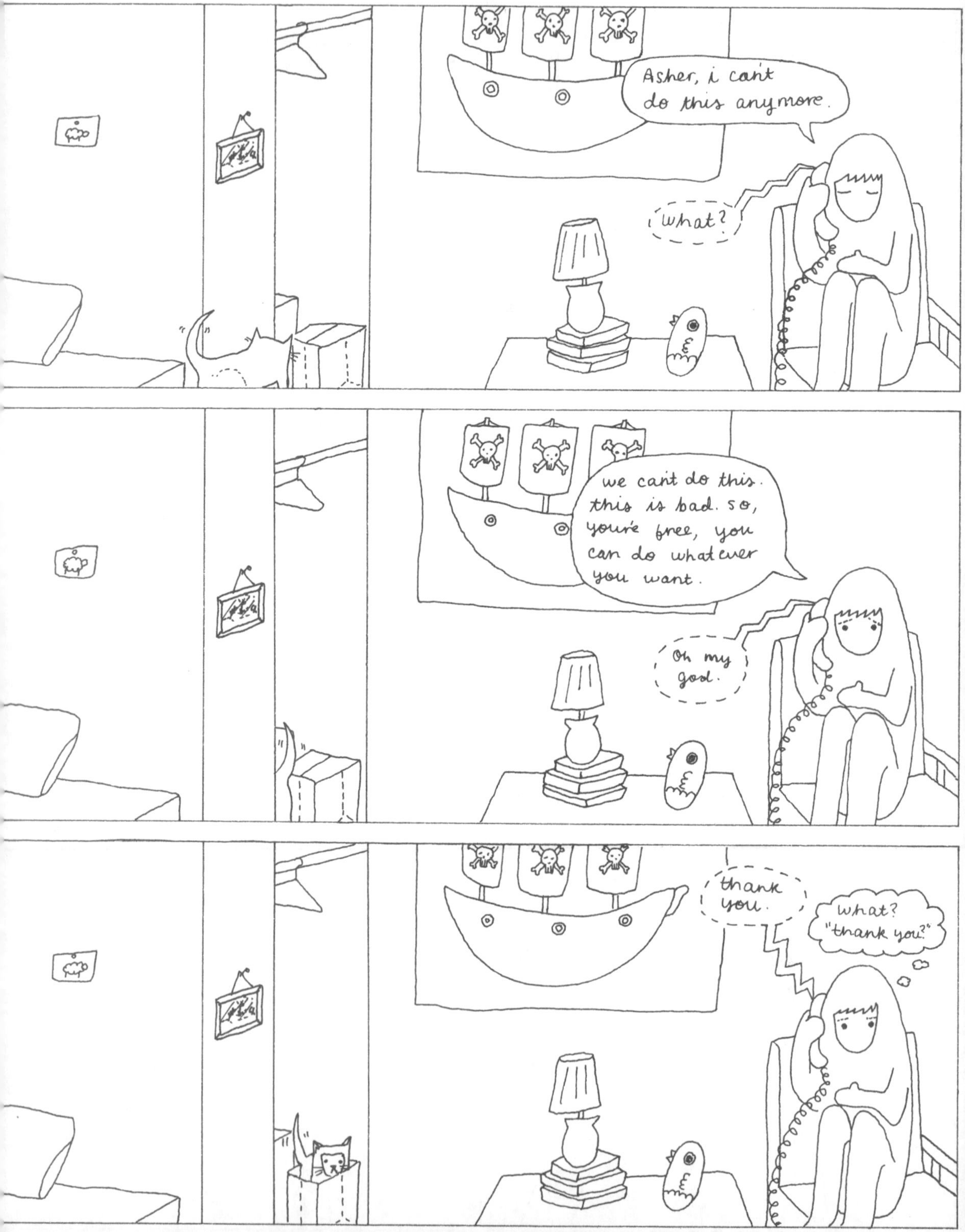
Asher, i can't do this anymore.
what?
we can't do this. this is bad. so, you're free, you can do whatever you want.
Oh my god.
thank you.
what? "thank you?"

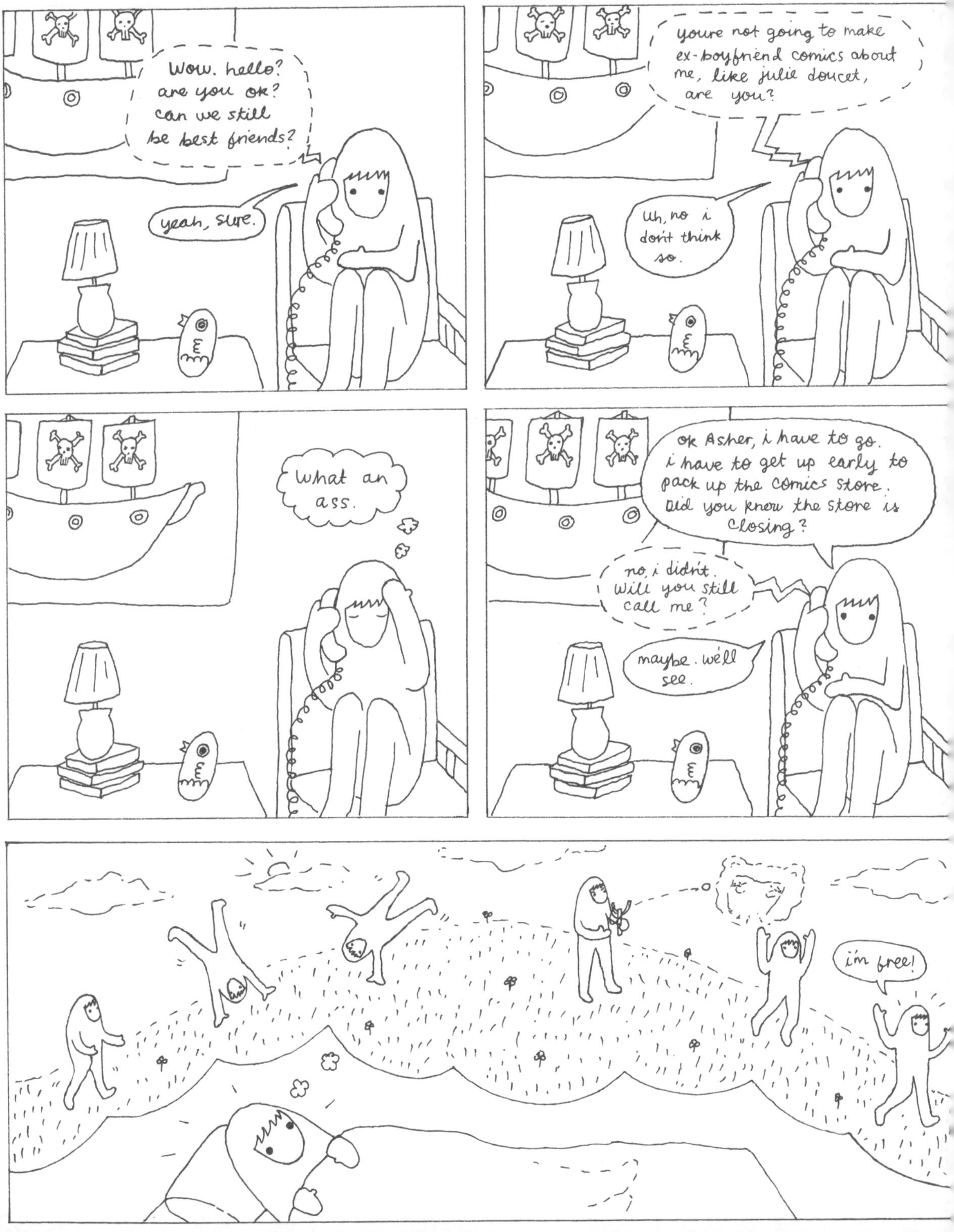
Wow. hello? are you ok? can we still be best friends?
yeah, sure.
youre not going to make ex-boyfriend comics about me, like julie doucet, are you?
uh, no i don't think so.
What an ass.
Ok Asher, i have to go. i have to get up early to pack up the Comics store. Did you know the store is closing?
no, i didn't. will you still call me?
maybe. we'll see.
i'm free!

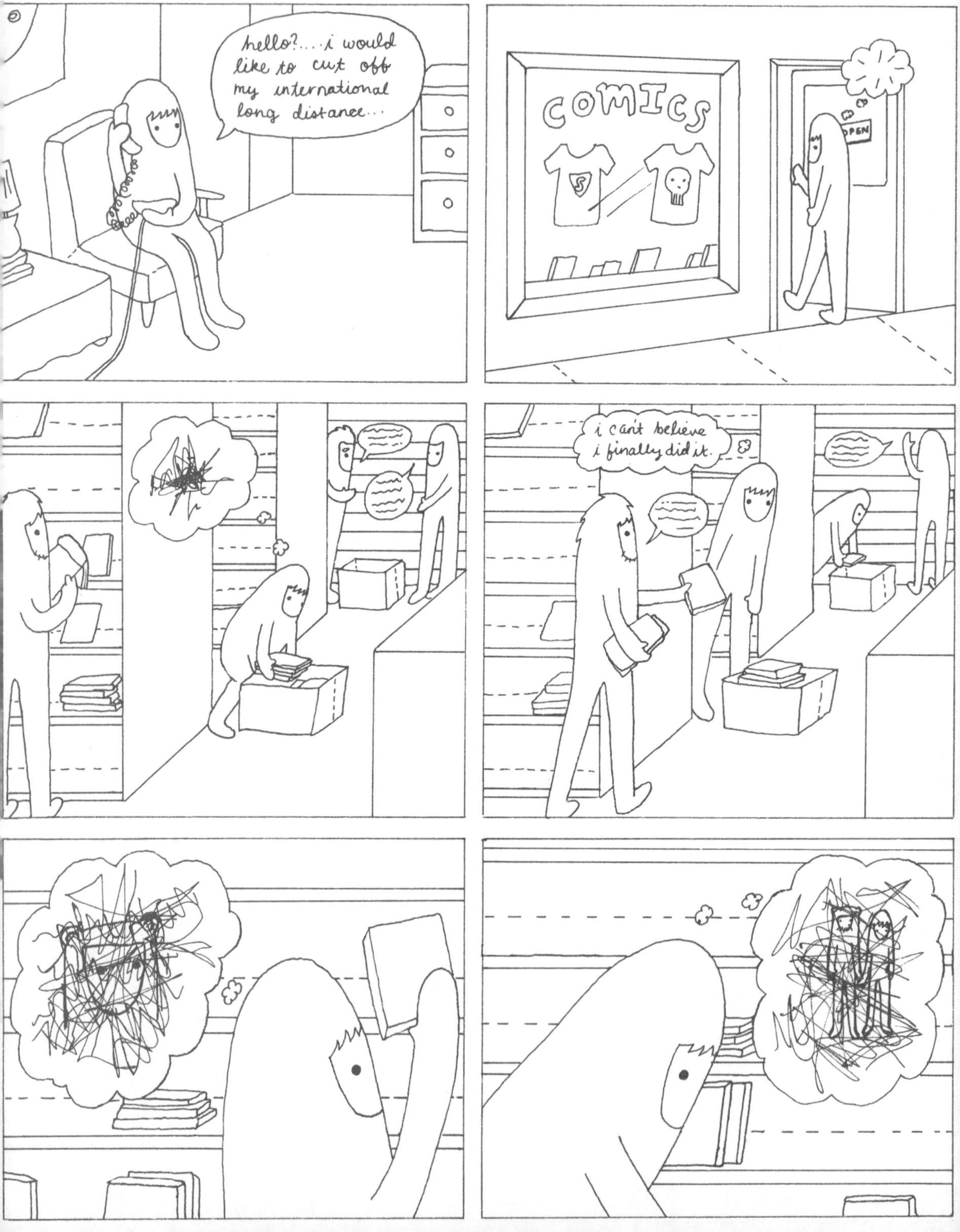
hello?.... i would like to cut off my international long distance...
COMICS
OPEN
i can't believe i finally did it.

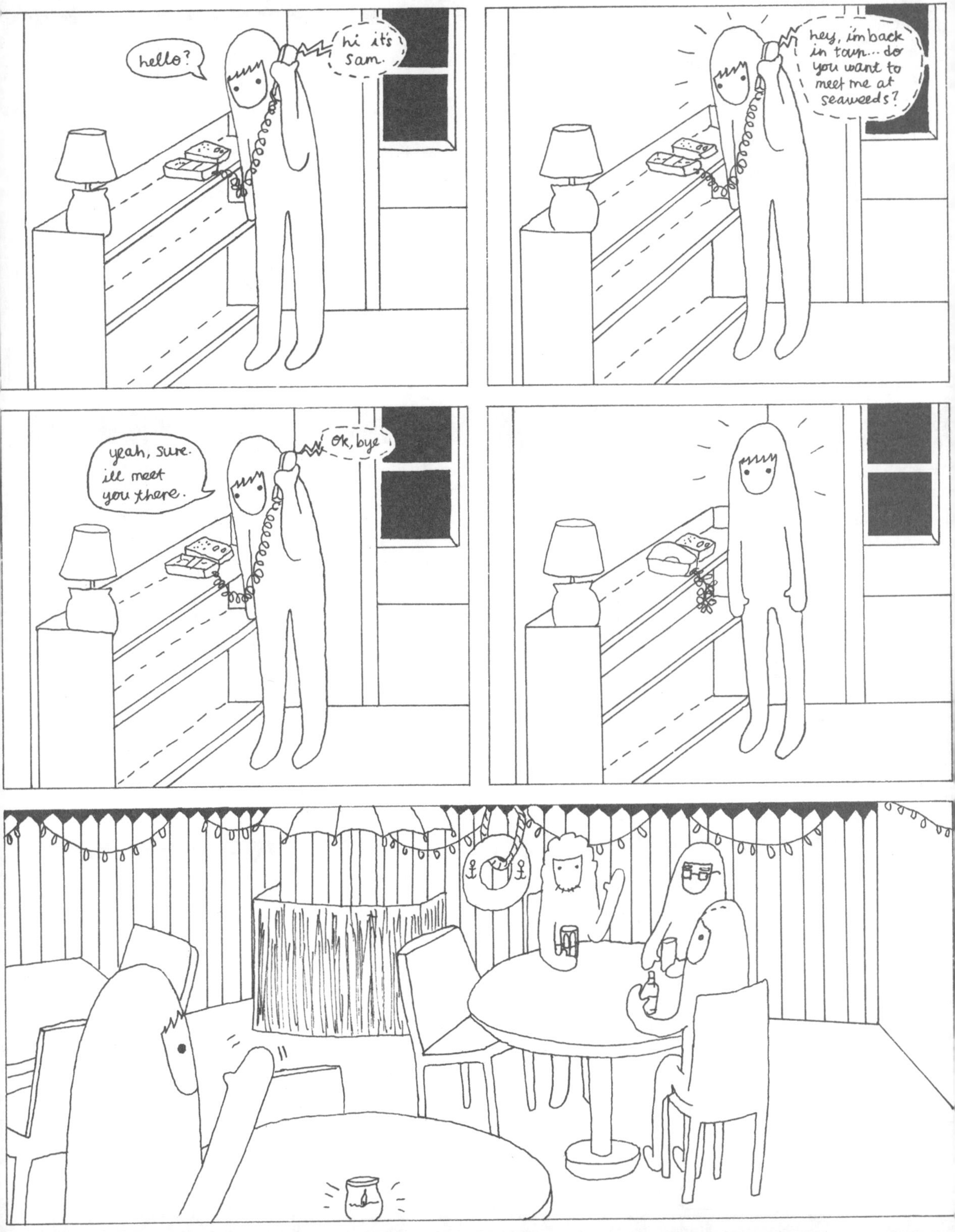
hello?
hi it's sam.
hey, im back in town... do you want to meet me at seaweeds?
yeah, sure. ill meet you there.
ok, bye

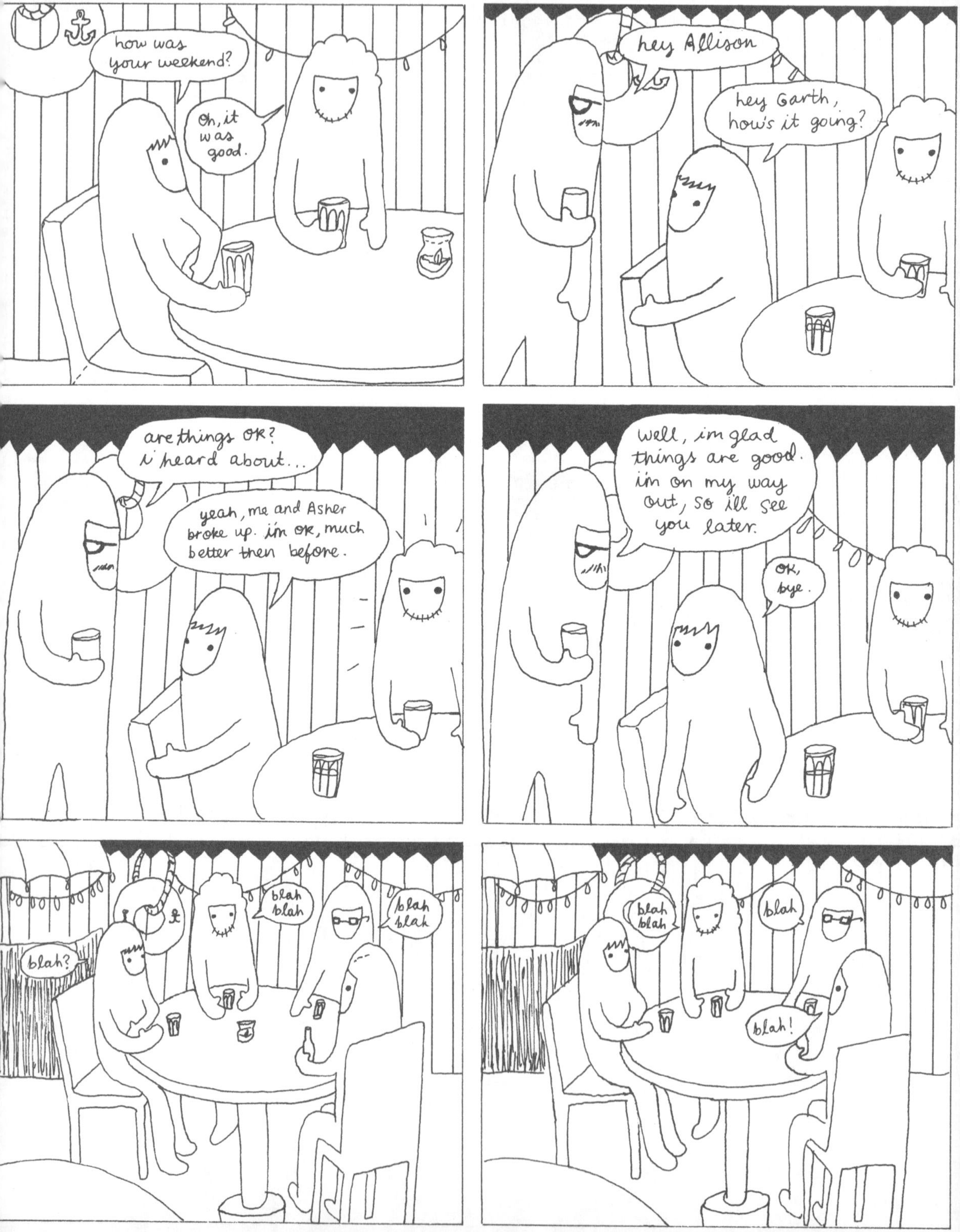
how was your weekend?
Oh, it was good.
hey Allison
hey Garth, how's it going?
are things OK? i heard about...
yeah, me and Asher broke up. im ok, much better then before.
well, im glad things are good. im on my way out, so ill see you later.
OK, bye.
blah blah
blah blah
blah?
blah blah
blah
blah!

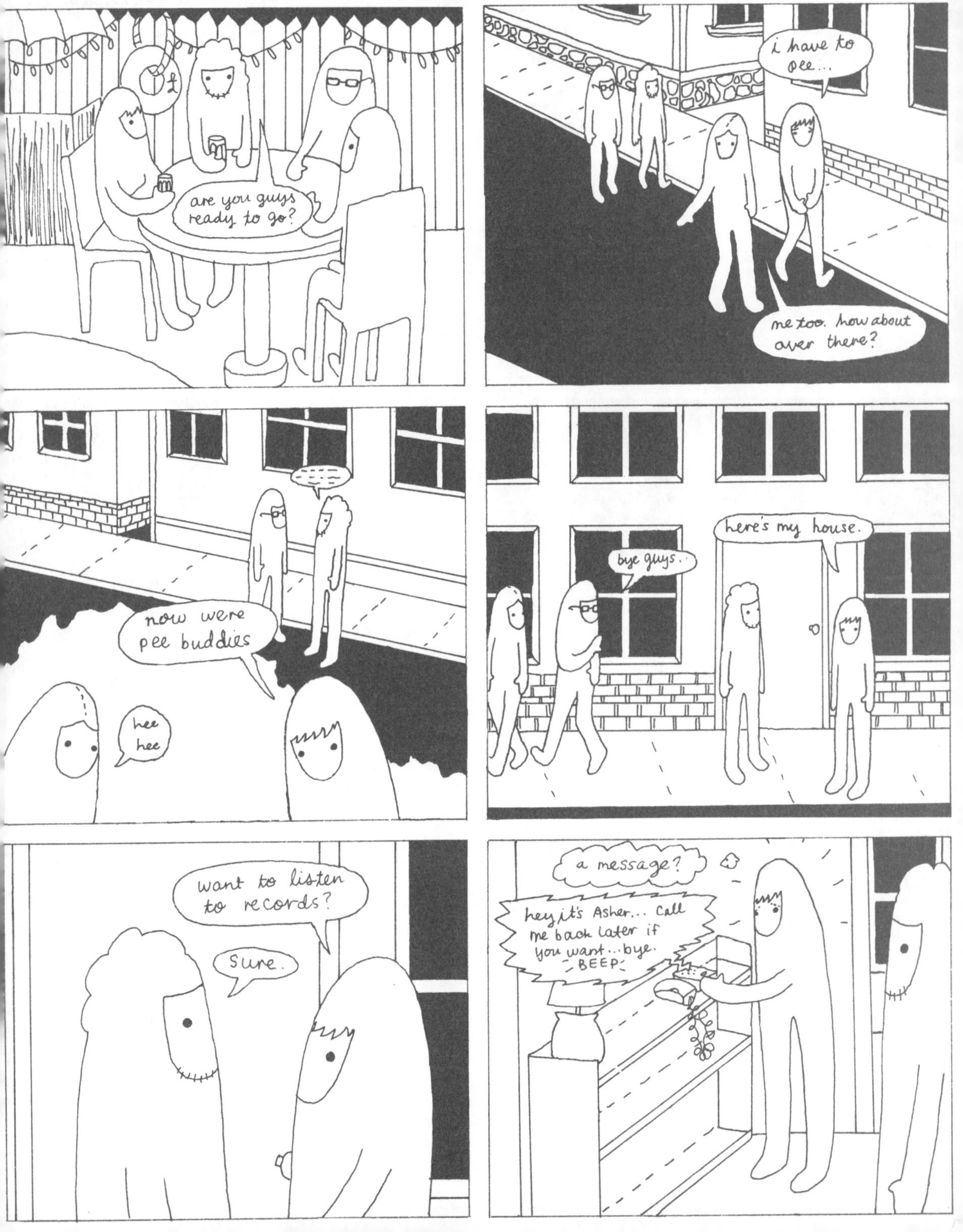
are you guys ready to go?
i have to pee...
me too. how about over there?
now were pee buddies
hee hee
here's my house.
bye guys..
want to listen to records?
Sure.
a message?
hey it's Asher... Call me back later if you want... bye.
BEEP

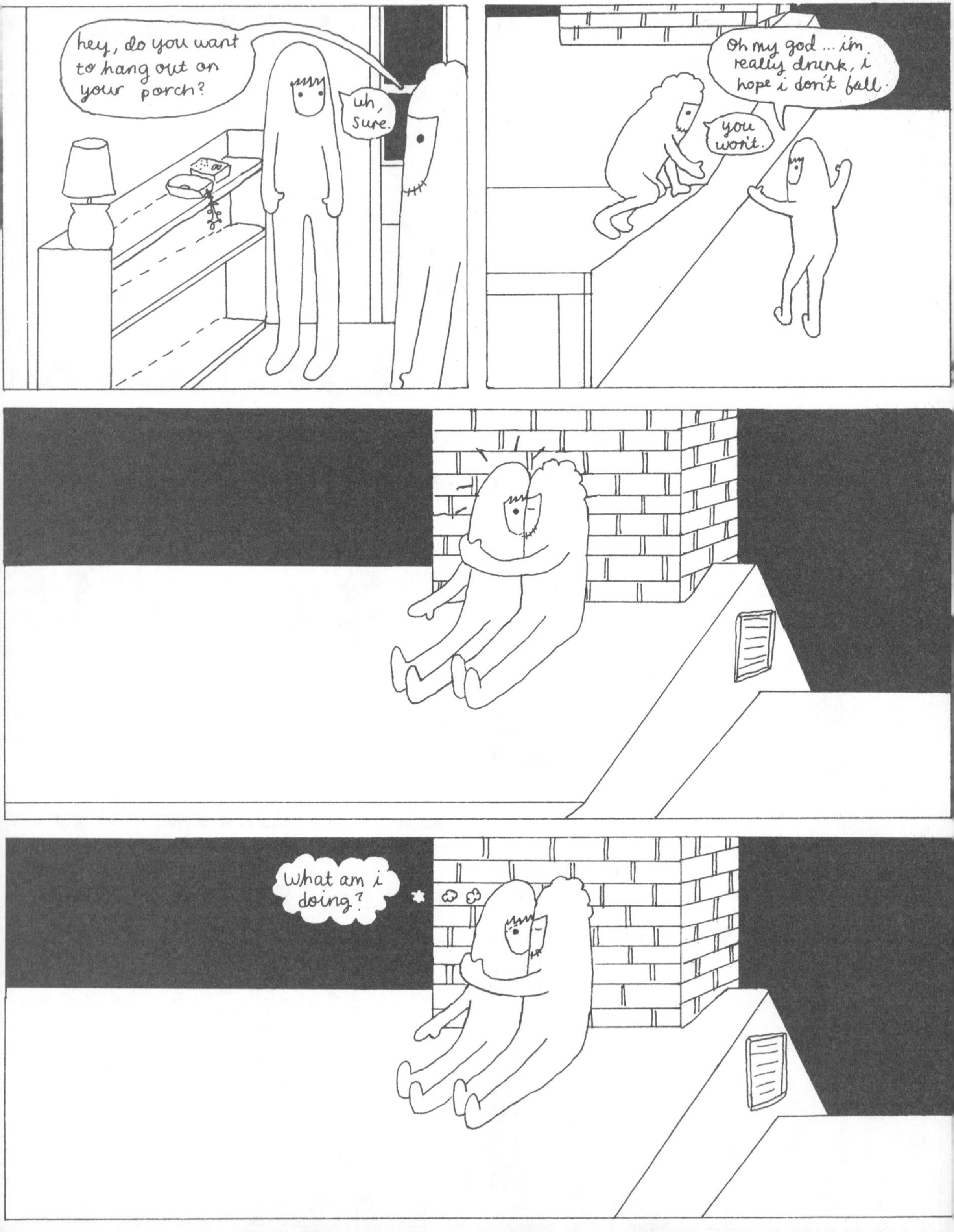
hey, do you want to hang out on your porch?
uh, sure.
Oh my god ... im really drunk, i hope i don't fall.
you won't.
What am i doing?

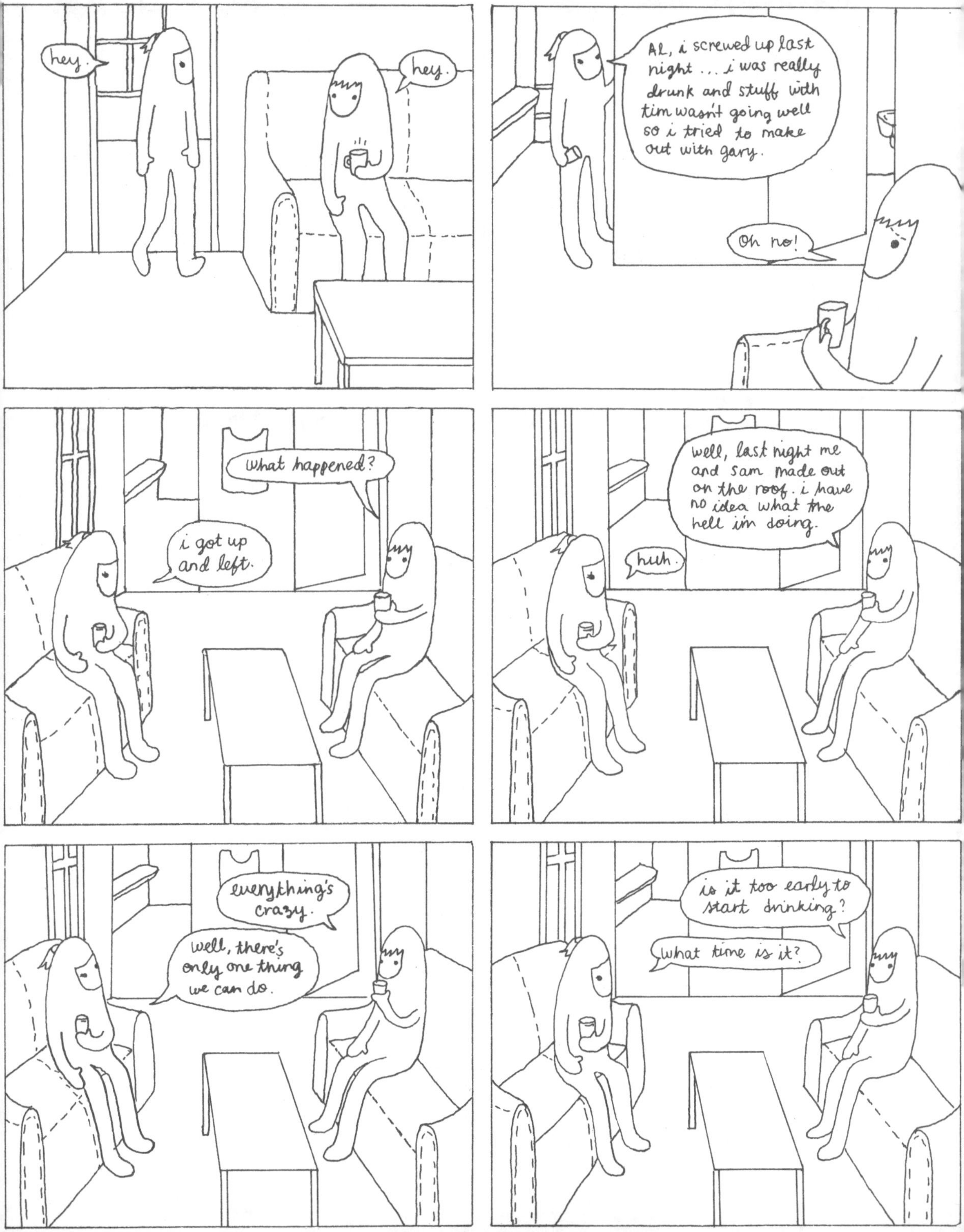
hey.
hey.
AL, i screwed up last night ... i was really drunk and stuff with tim wasn't going well so i tried to make out with gary.
Oh no!
What happened?
i got up and left.
well, last night me and sam made out on the roof. i have no idea what the hell im doing.
huh.
everything's crazy.
well, there's only one thing we can do.
is it too early to start drinking?
What time is it?

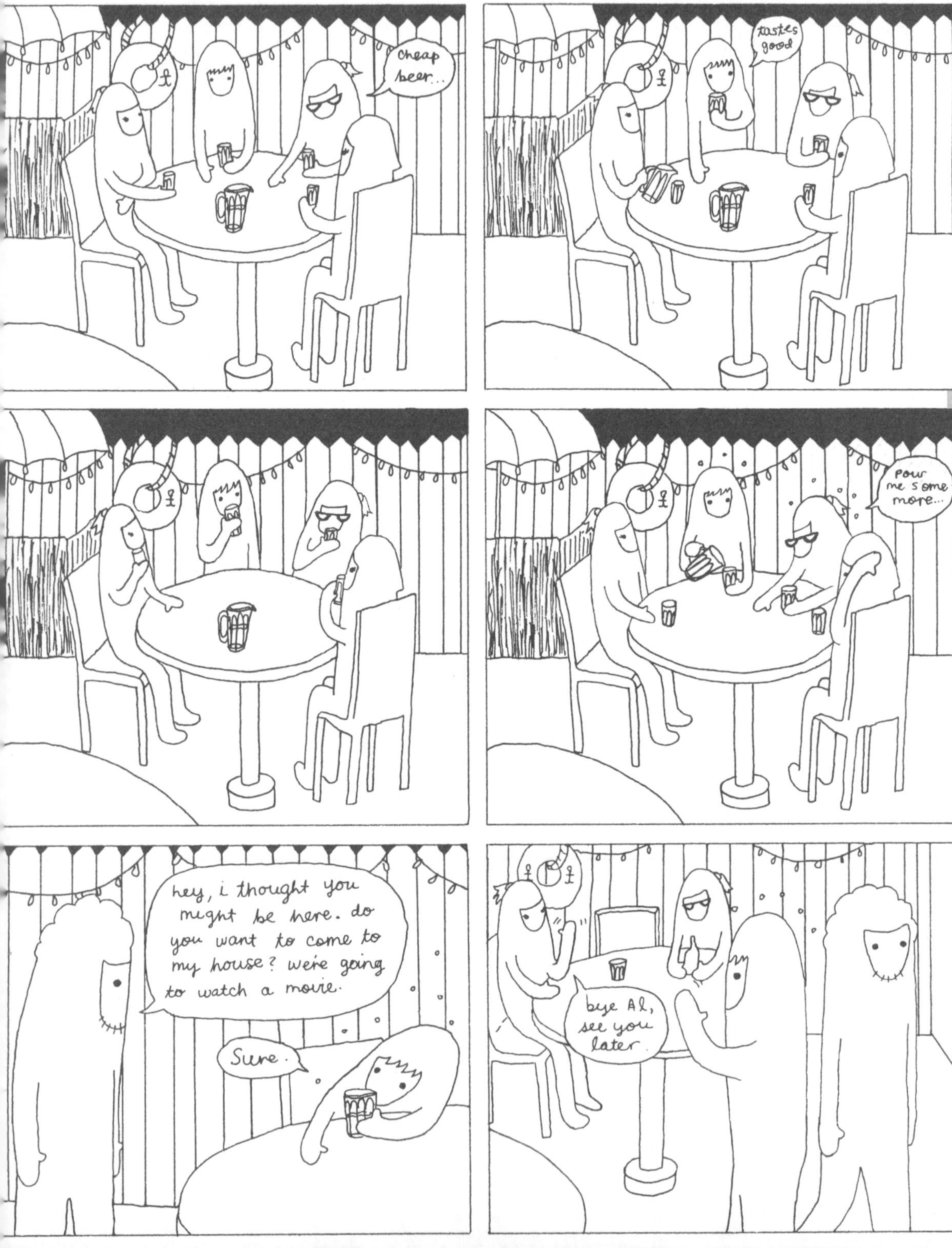
Cheap beer...
tastes good
pour me some more...
hey, i thought you might be here. do you want to come to my house? we're going to watch a movie.
Sure.
bye Al, see you later.

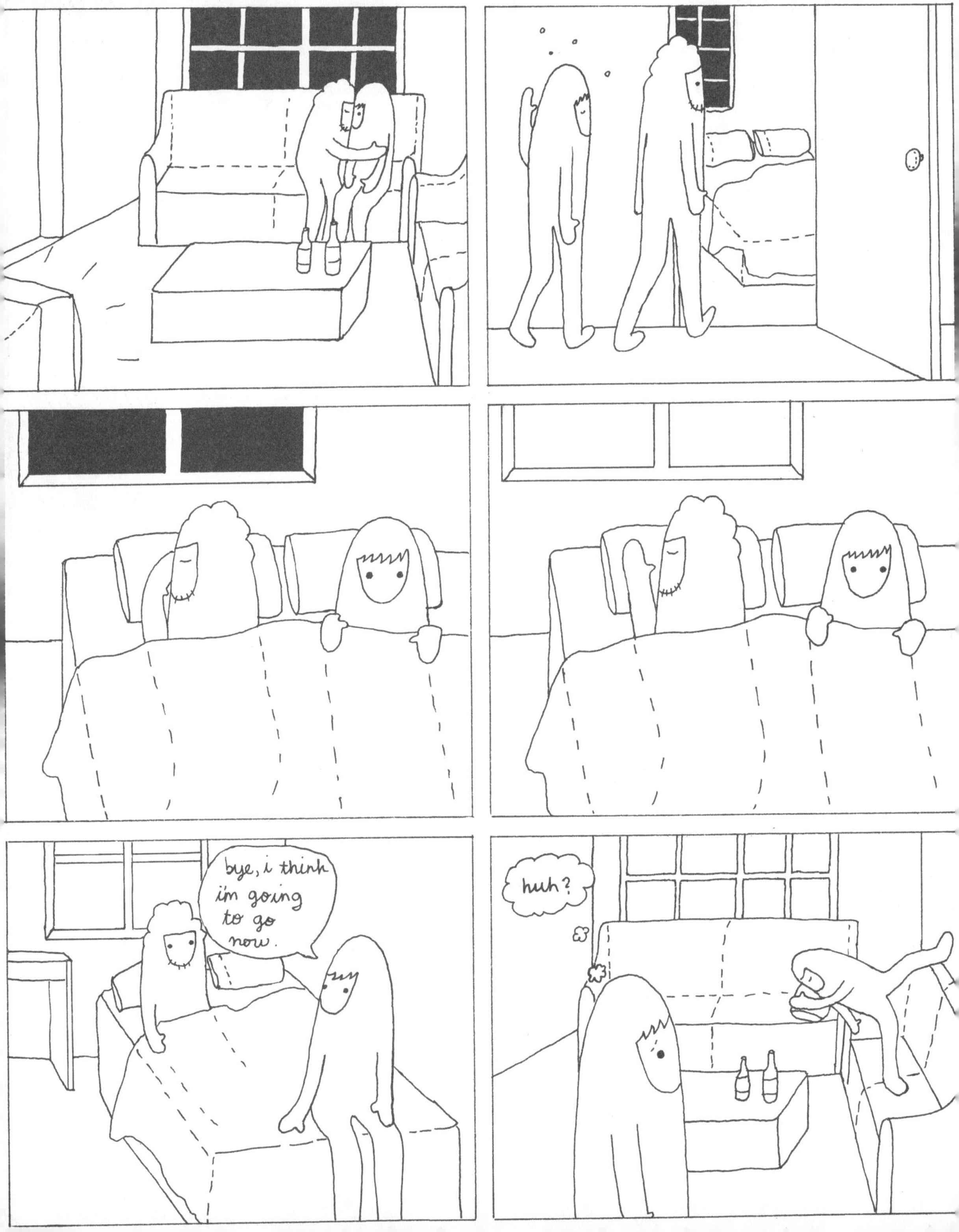
bye, i think i'm going to go now.
huh?

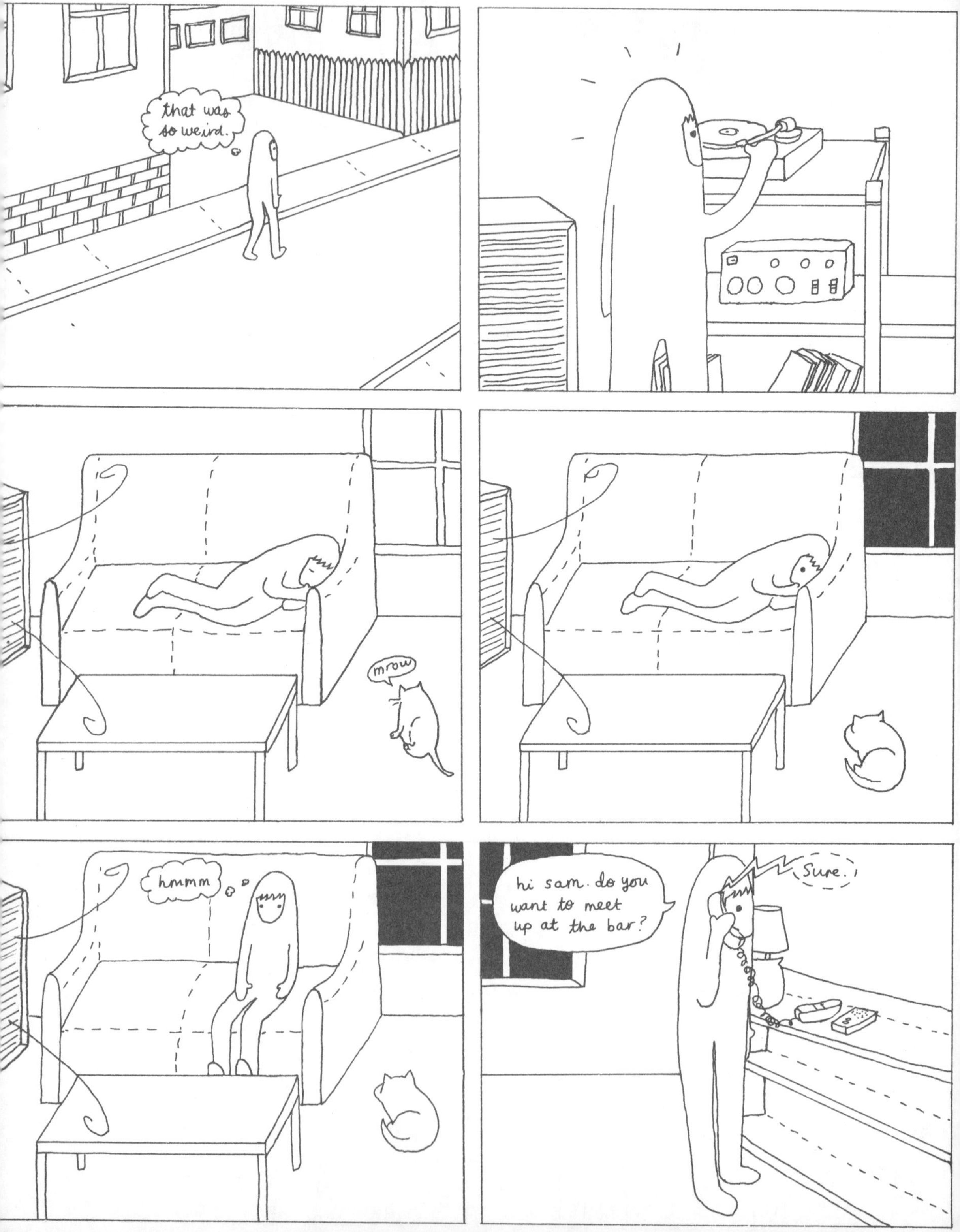

that was so weird.
mrow
hmmm
hi sam. do you want to meet up at the bar?
Sure.

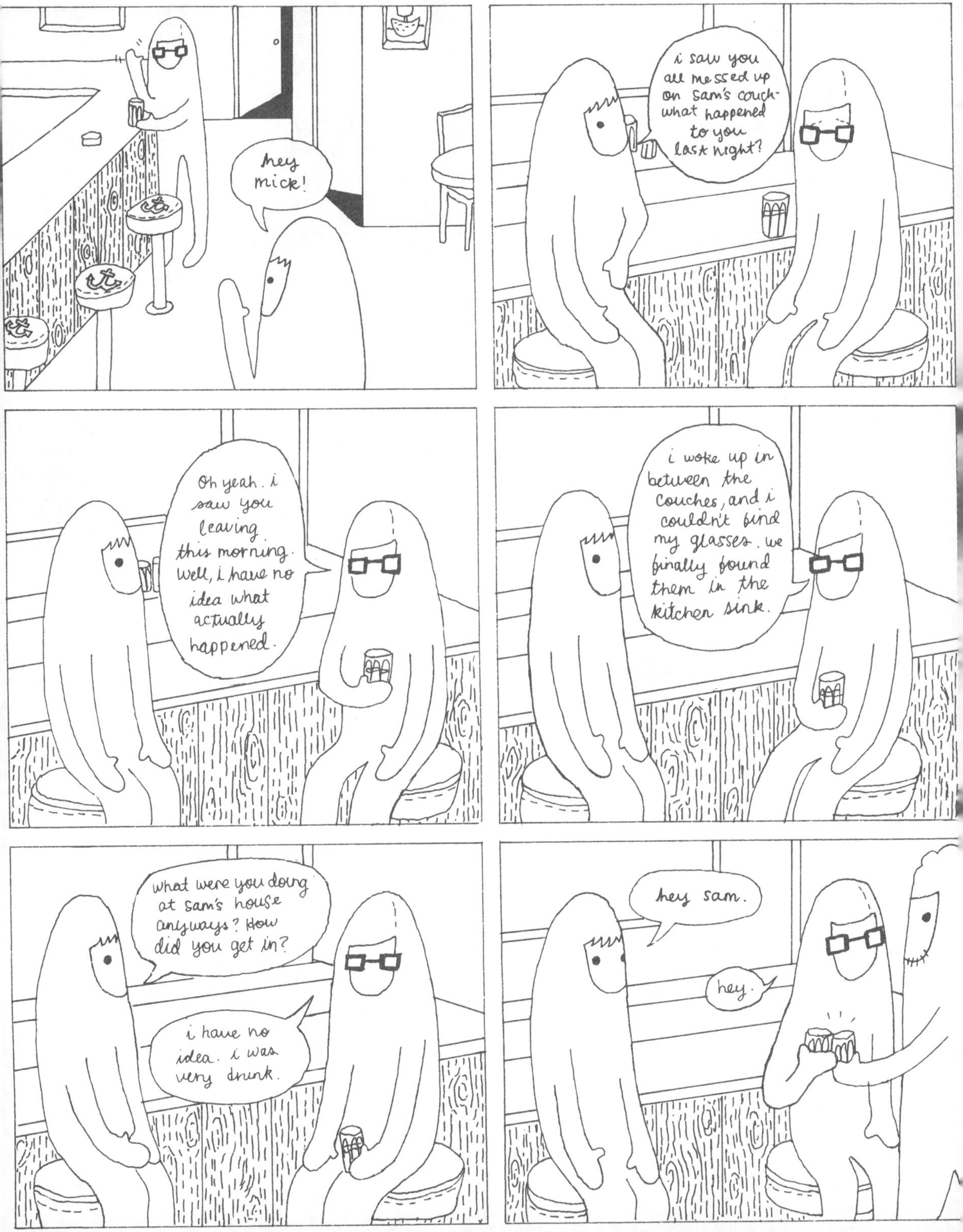
hey mick!
i saw you all messed up on sam's couch- what happened to you last night?
Oh yeah. i saw you leaving this morning. Well, i have no idea what actually happened.
i woke up in between the couches, and i couldn't find my glasses. we finally found them in the kitchen sink.
what were you doing at sam's house anyways? How did you get in?
i have no idea. i was very drunk.
hey sam.
hey.

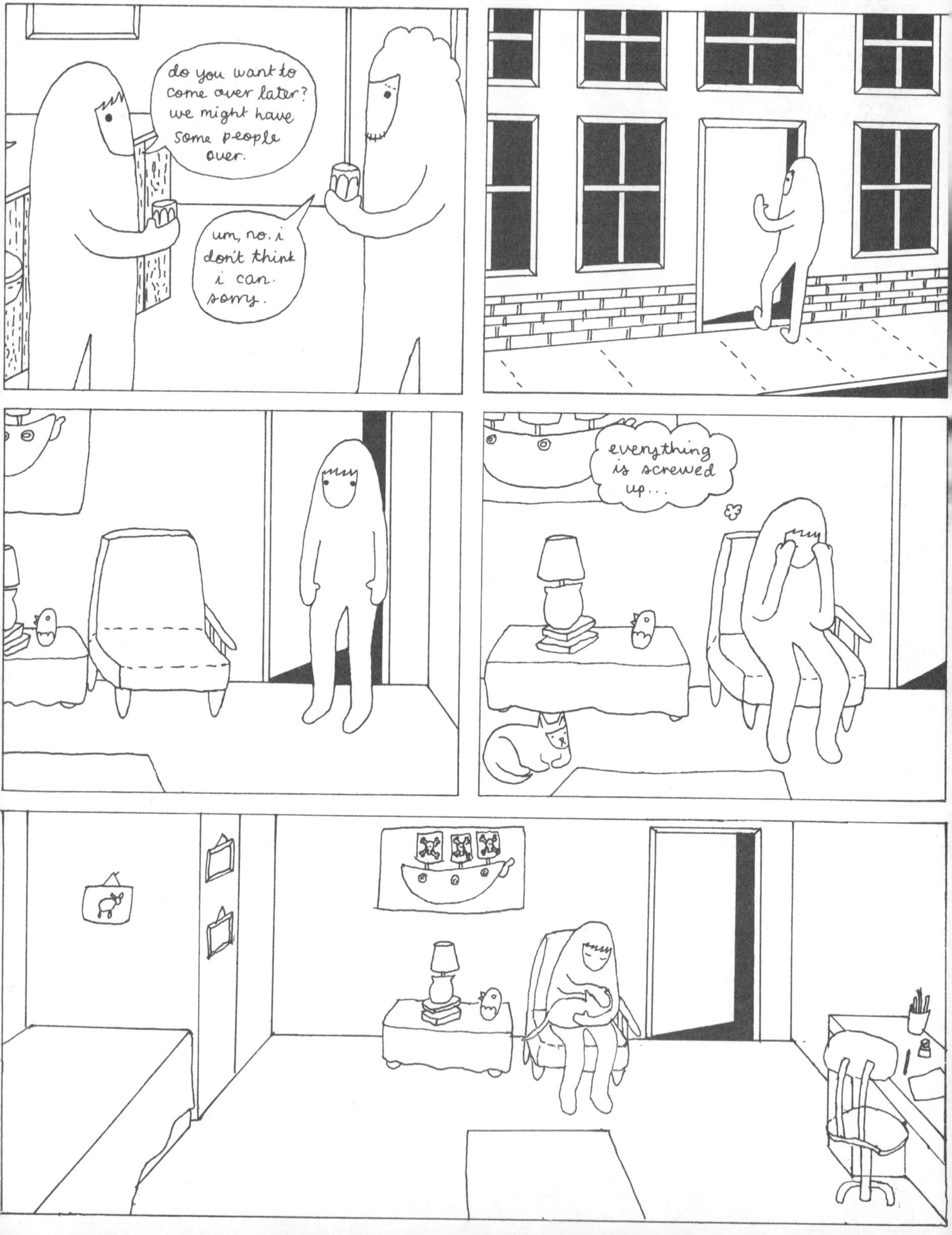
do you want to come over later? we might have some people over.
um, no. i don't think i can. sorry.
everything is screwed up...

August

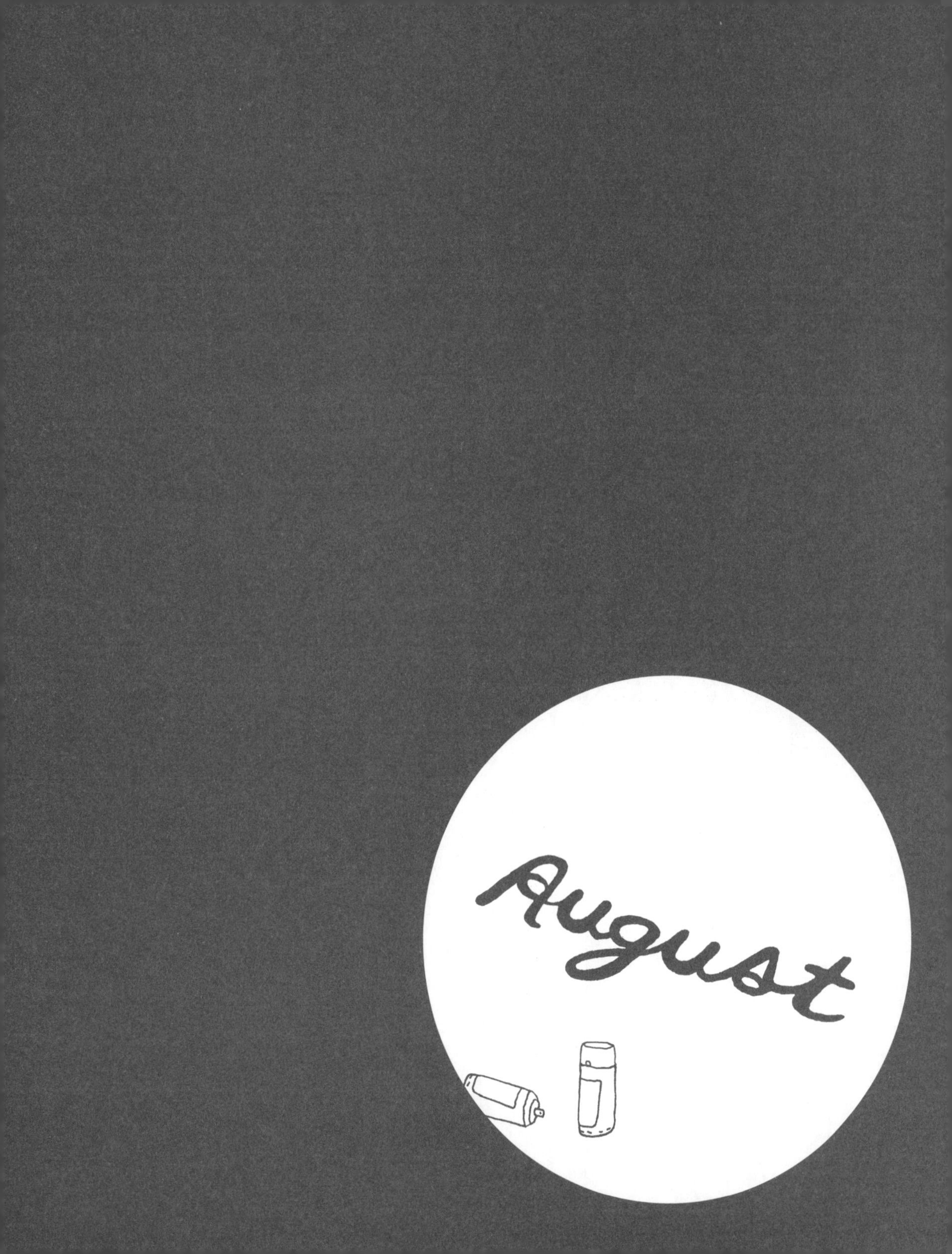

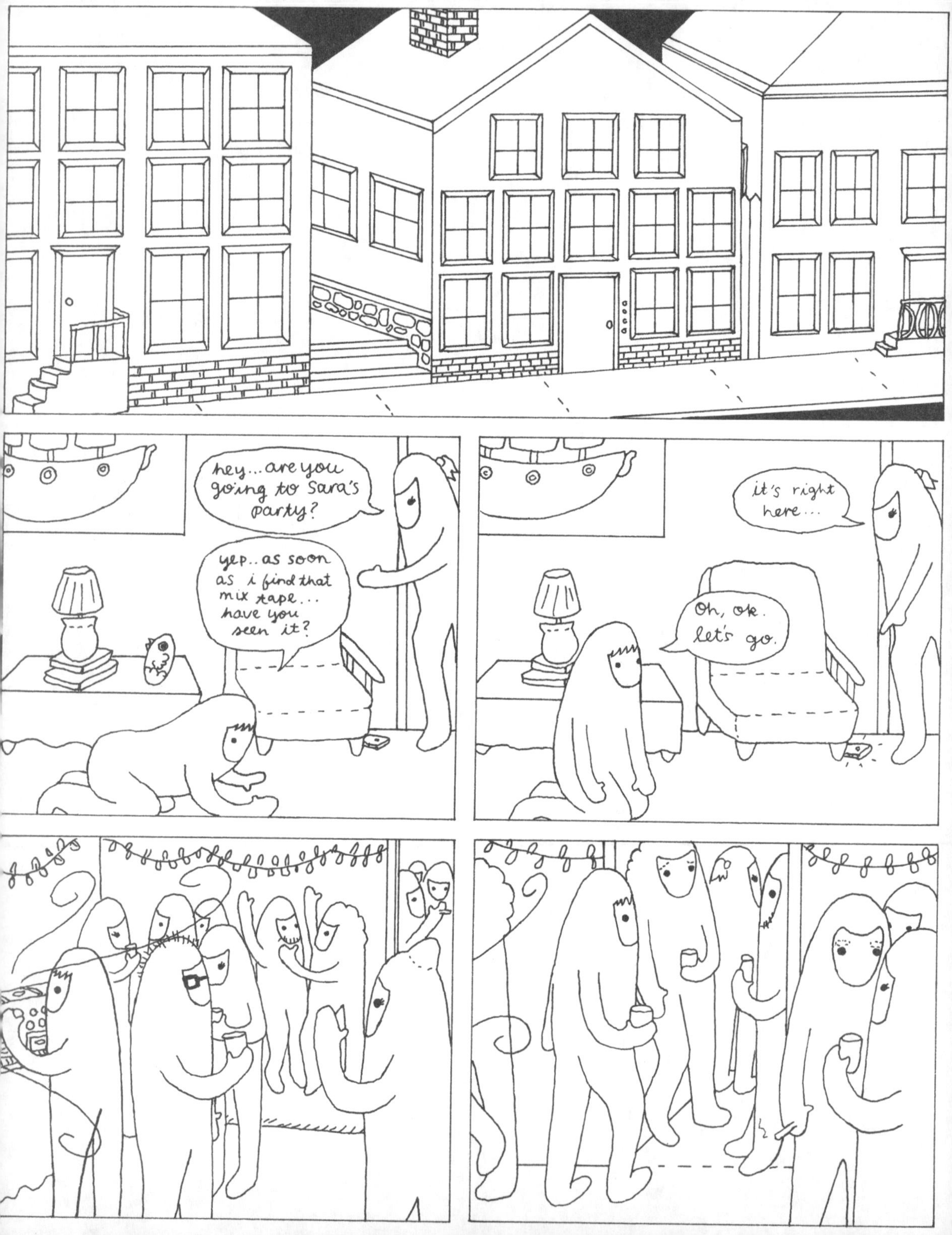
hey... are you going to Sara's party?
yep.. as soon as i find that mix tape... have you seen it?
it's right here...
Oh, ok. let's go.

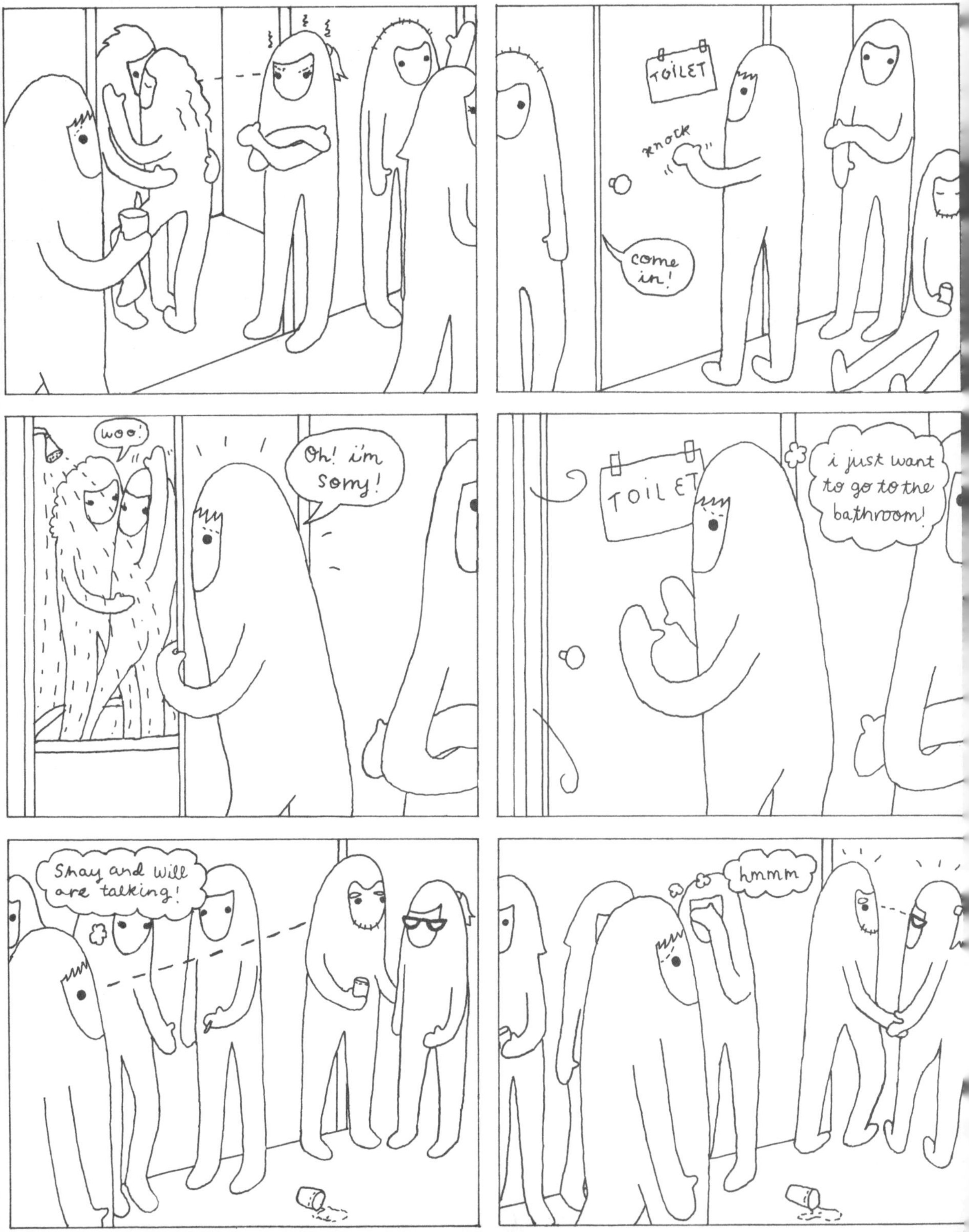

TOILET
knock
come in!
woo!
Oh! i'm sorry!
TOILET
i just want to go to the bathroom!
Shay and will are talking!
hmmm

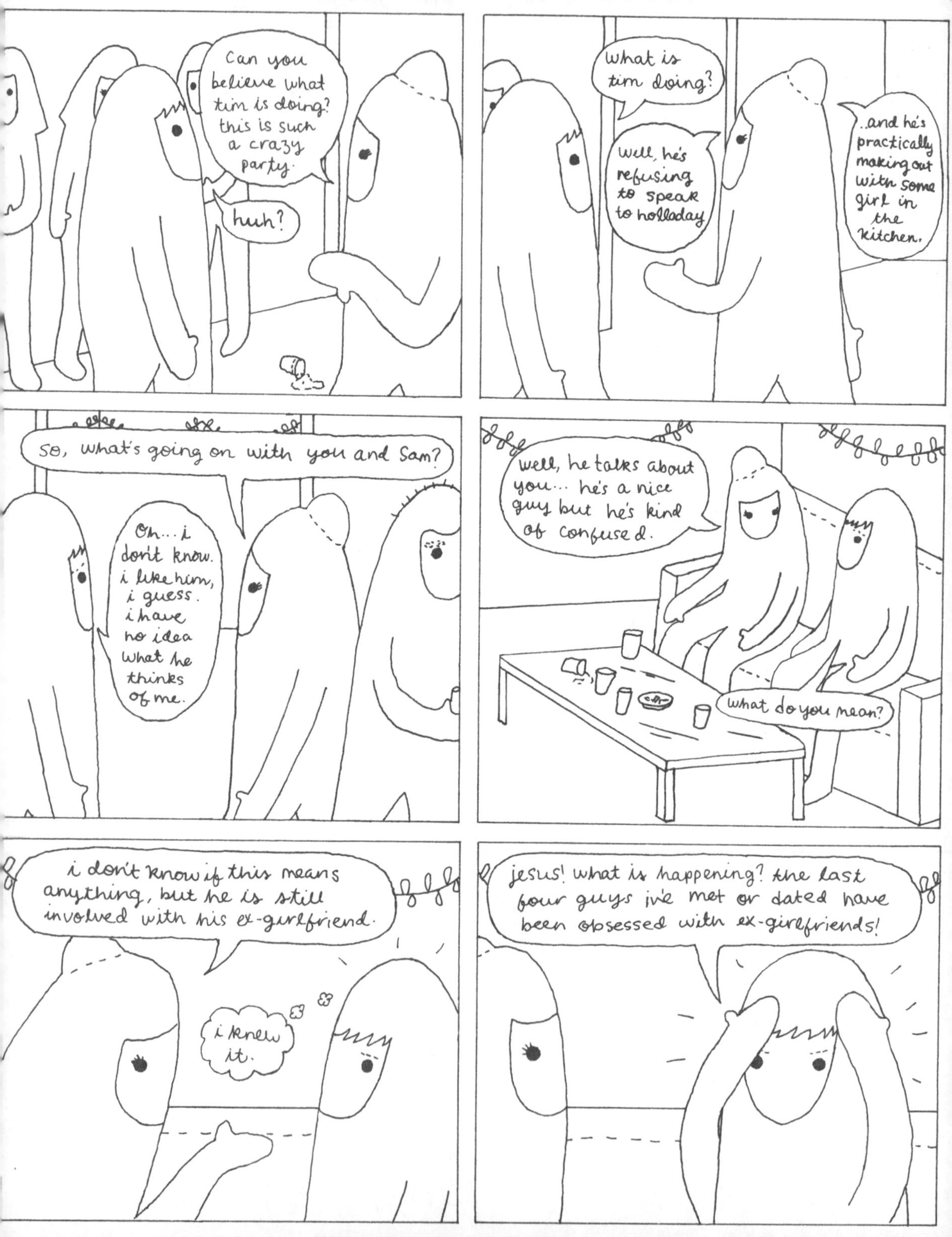
Can you believe what tim is doing? this is such a crazy party.
huh?
What is tim doing?
Well, he's refusing to speak to holladay
..and he's practically making out with some girl in the kitchen.
So, what's going on with you and Sam?
Oh... i don't know. i like him, i guess. i have no idea what he thinks of me.
Well, he talks about you... he's a nice guy but he's kind of confused.
What do you mean?
i don't know if this means anything, but he is still involved with his ex-girlfriend.
i knew it.
jesus! what is happening? the last four guys i've met or dated have been obsessed with ex-girlfriends!

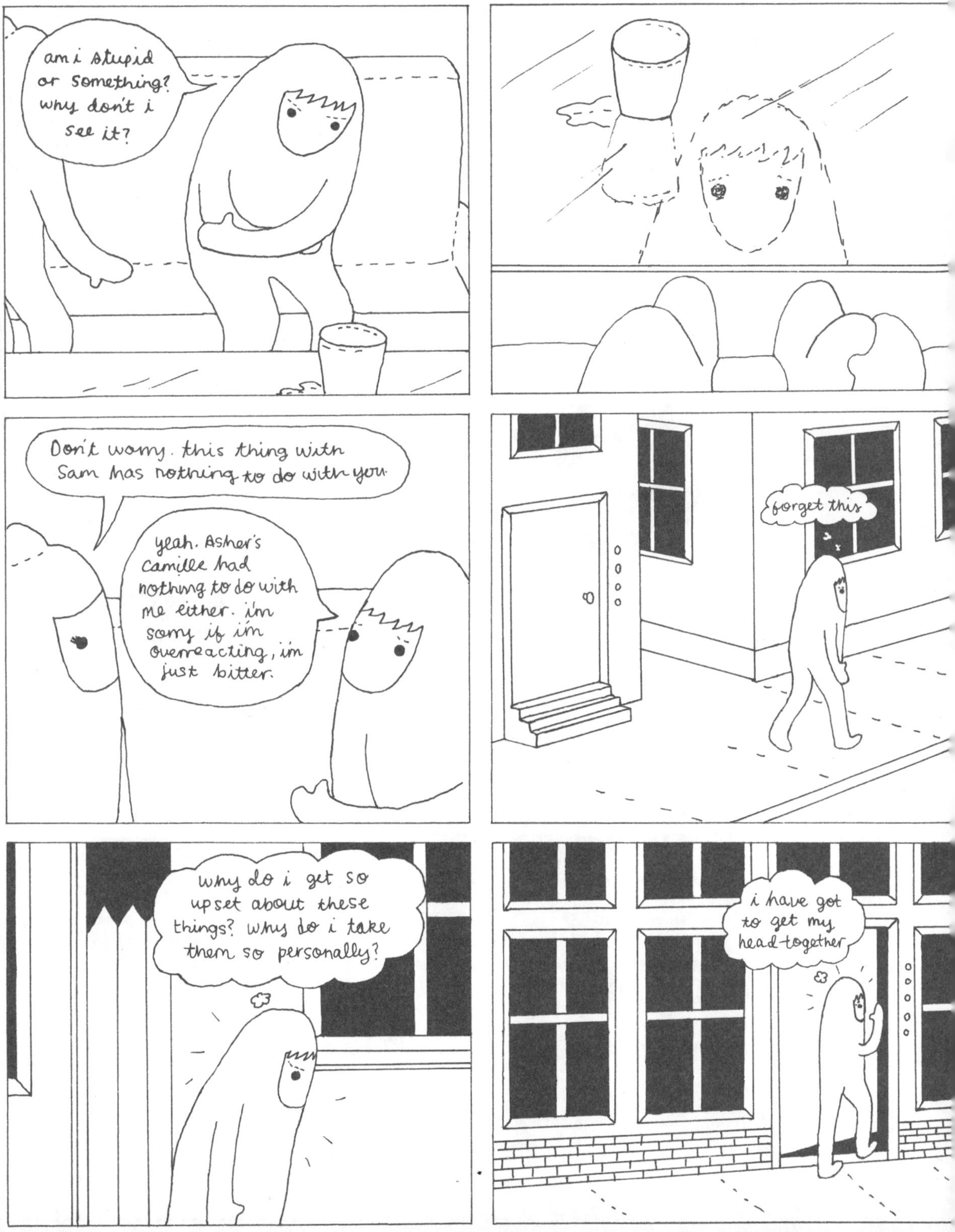
am i stupid or something? why don't i see it?
Don't worry. this thing with Sam has nothing to do with you.
yeah. Asher's Camille had nothing to do with me either. i'm sorry if i'm overreacting, i'm just bitter.
forget this
why do i get so upset about these things? why do i take them so personally?
i have got to get my head together

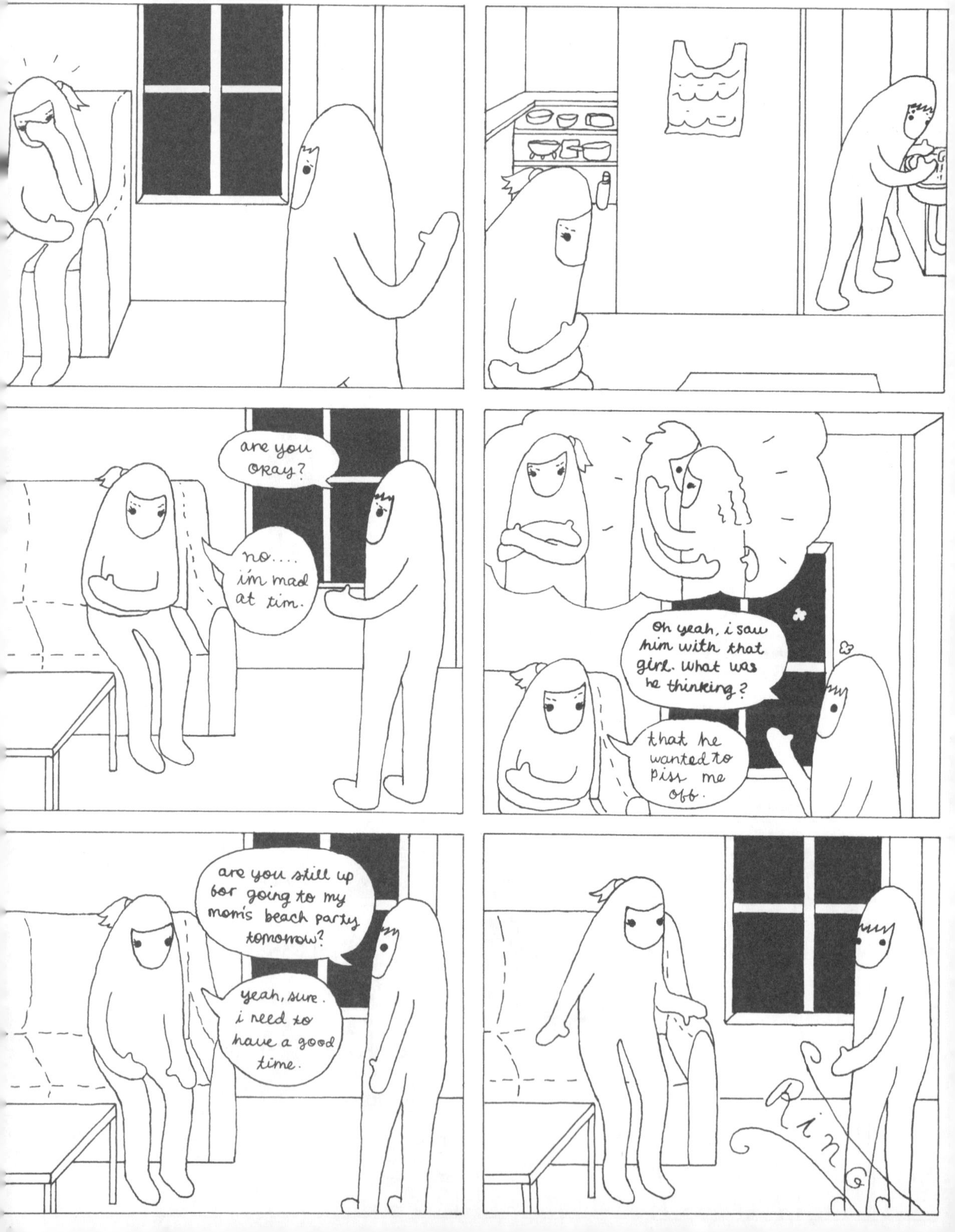
are you okay?
no.... i'm mad at tim.
Oh yeah, i saw him with that girl. What was he thinking?
that he wanted to piss me off.
are you still up for going to my mom's beach party tomorrow?
yeah, sure. i need to have a good time.
Ring

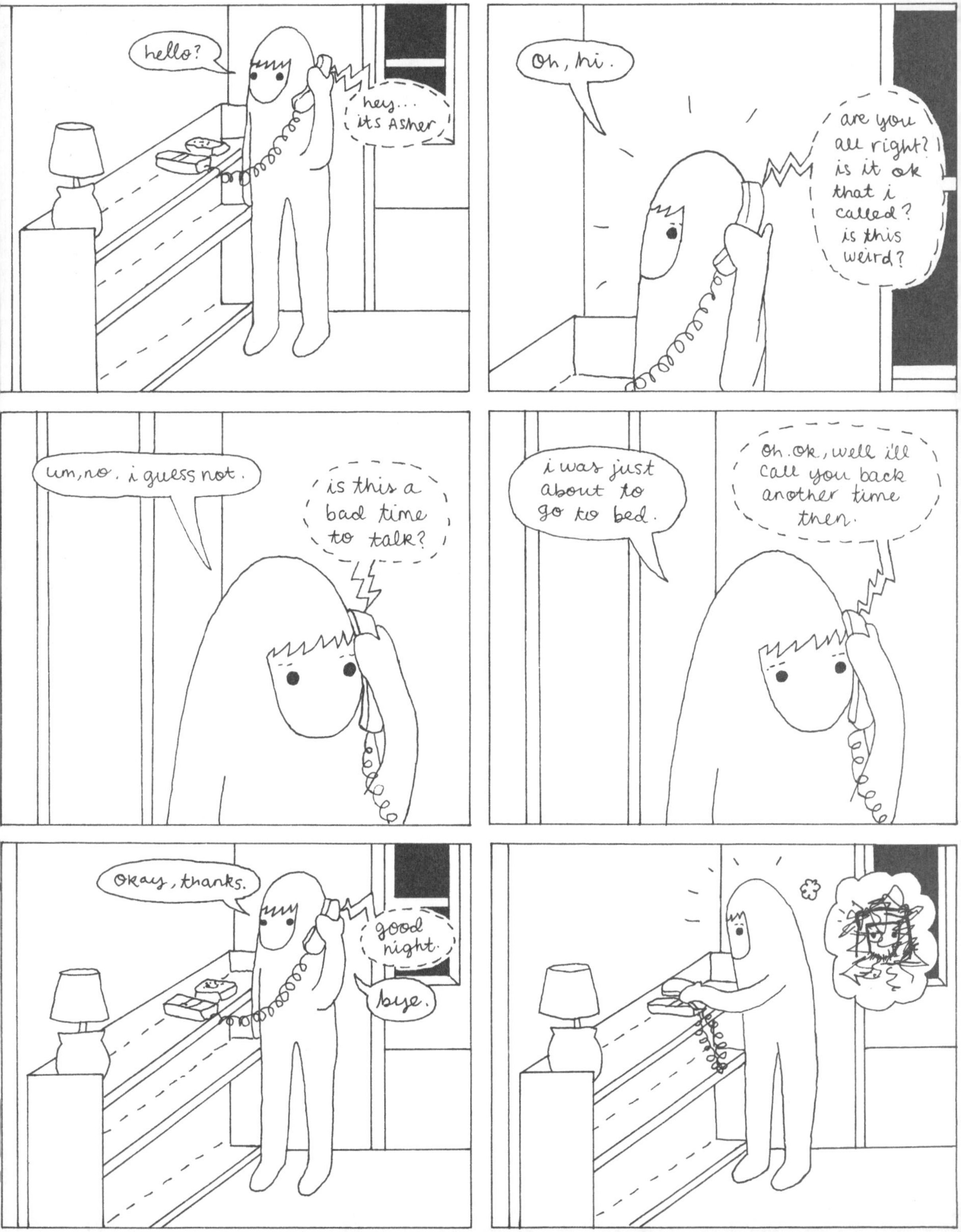
hello?
hey... its Asher
Oh, hi.
are you all right? is it ok that i called? is this weird?
um, no. i guess not.
is this a bad time to talk?
i was just about to go to bed.
Oh. ok, well i'll call you back another time then.
Okay, thanks.
good night.
bye.

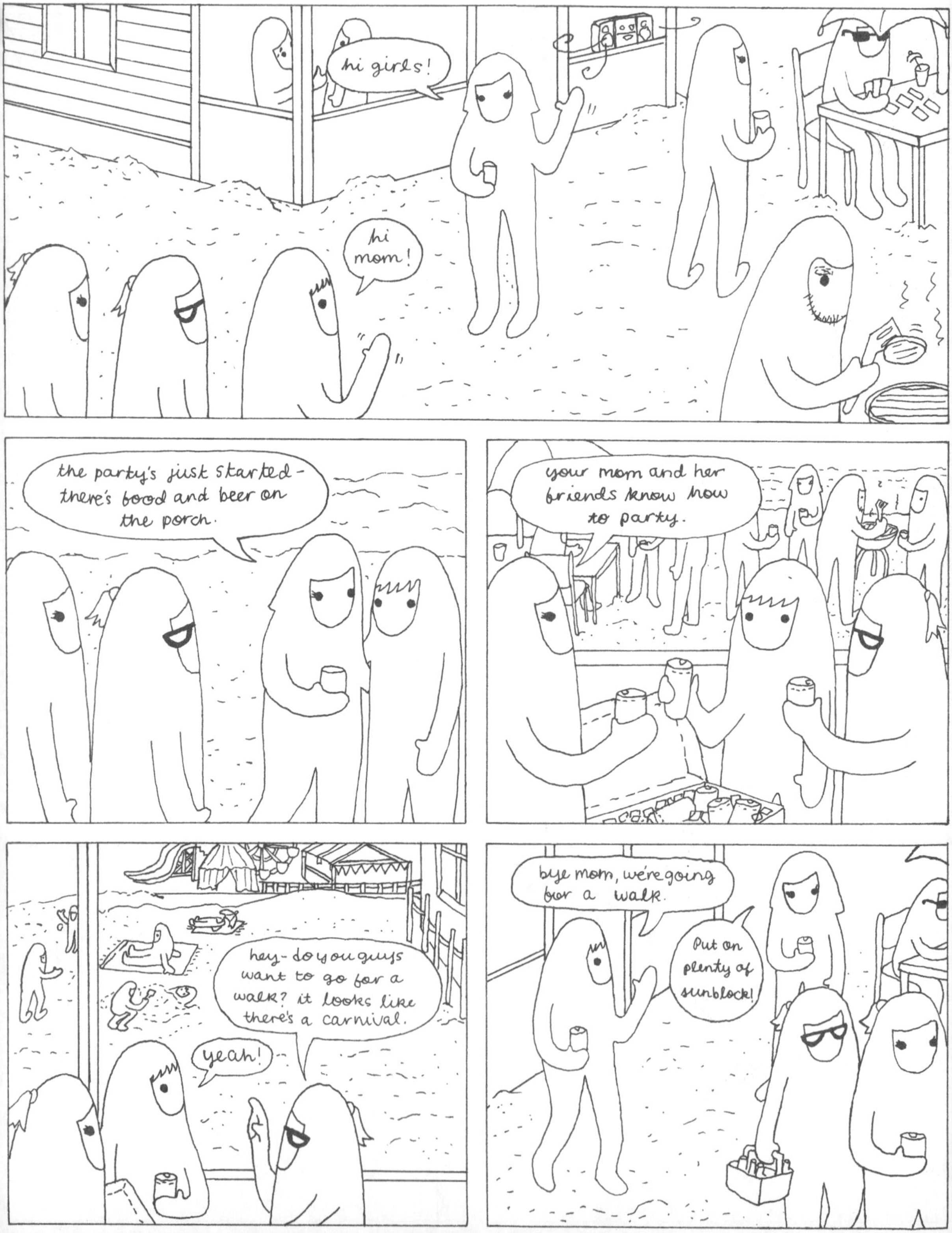
hi girls!
hi mom!
the party's just started - there's food and beer on the porch.
your mom and her friends know how to party.
hey - do you guys want to go for a walk? it looks like there's a carnival.
yeah!
bye mom, we're going for a walk.
Put on plenty of sunblock!

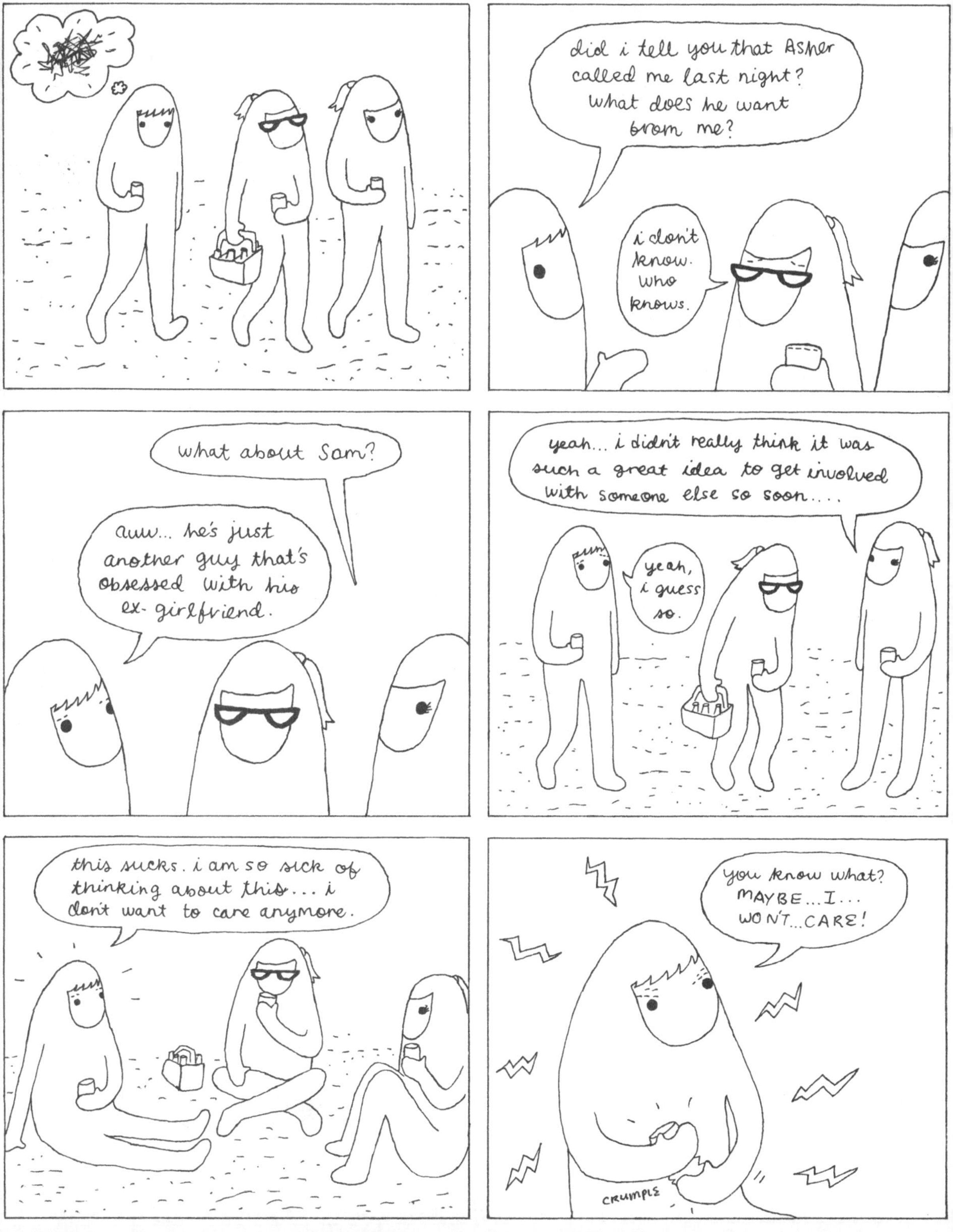
did i tell you that Asher called me last night? What does he want from me?
i don't know. Who knows.
what about Sam?
aww... he's just another guy that's obsessed with his ex-girlfriend.
yeah... i didn't really think it was such a great idea to get involved with someone else so soon....
yeah, i guess so.
this sucks. i am so sick of thinking about this... i don't want to care anymore.
you know what? MAYBE... I... WON'T... CARE!
CRUMPLE

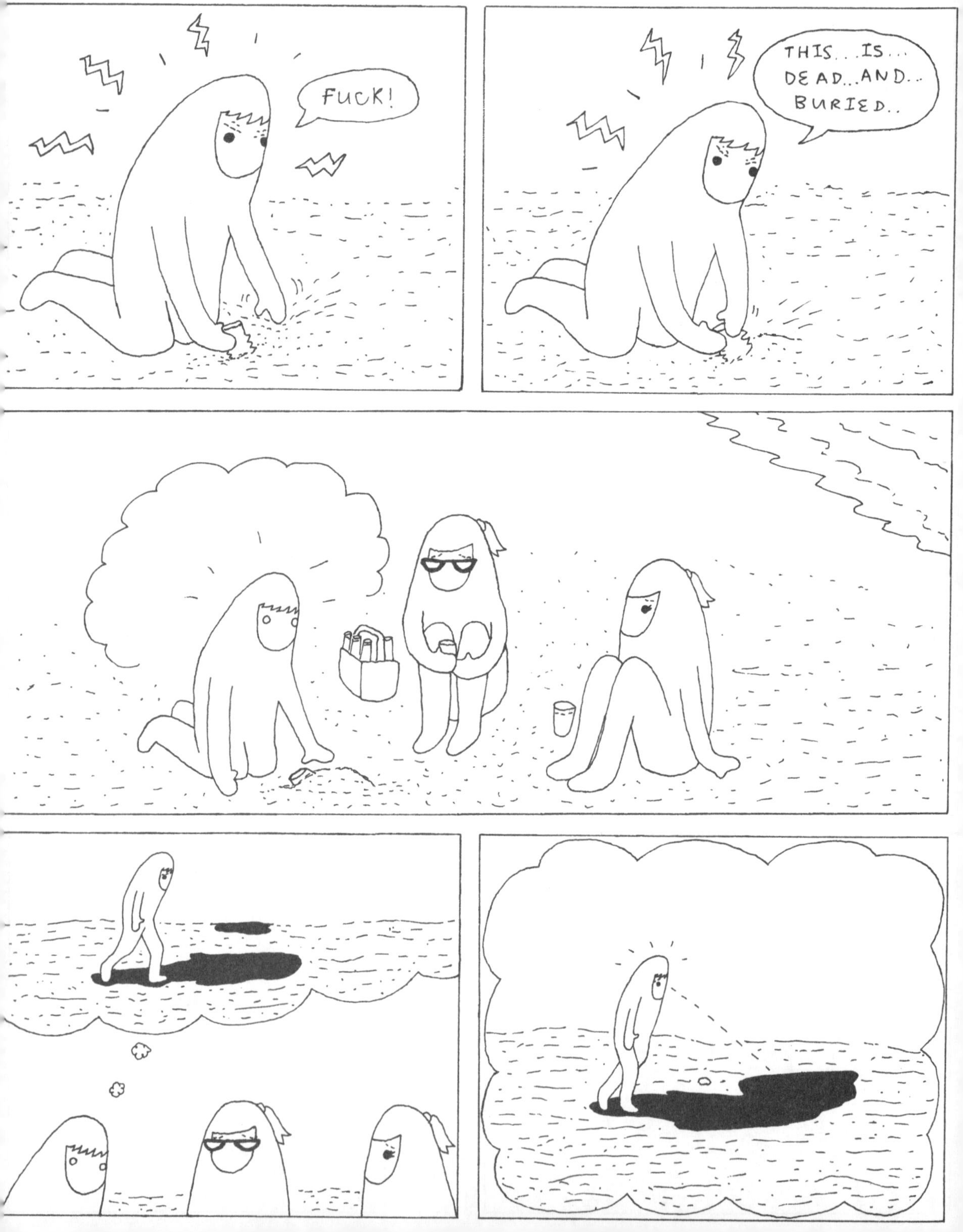
FUCK!
THIS... IS... DEAD... AND... BURIED..

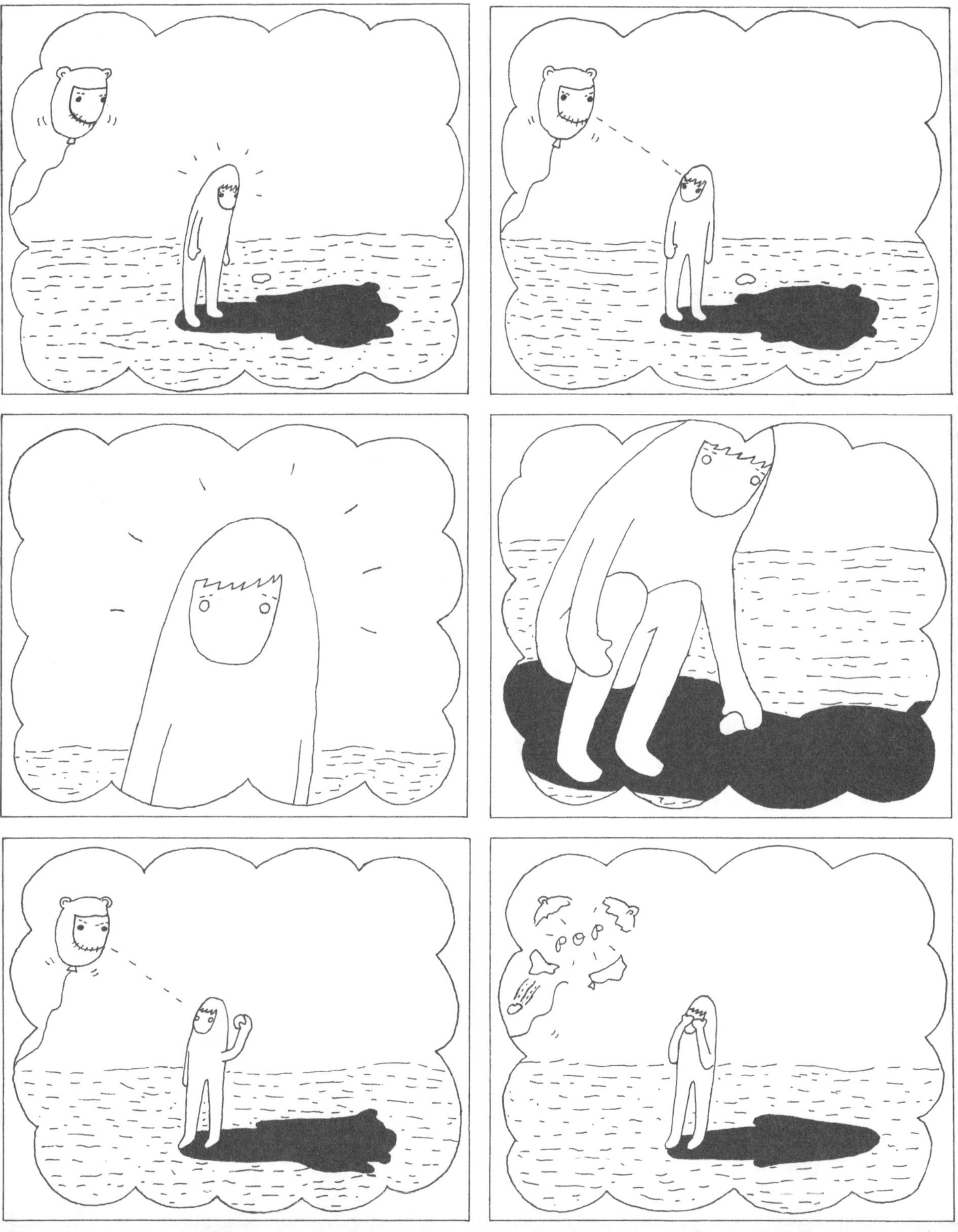
POP

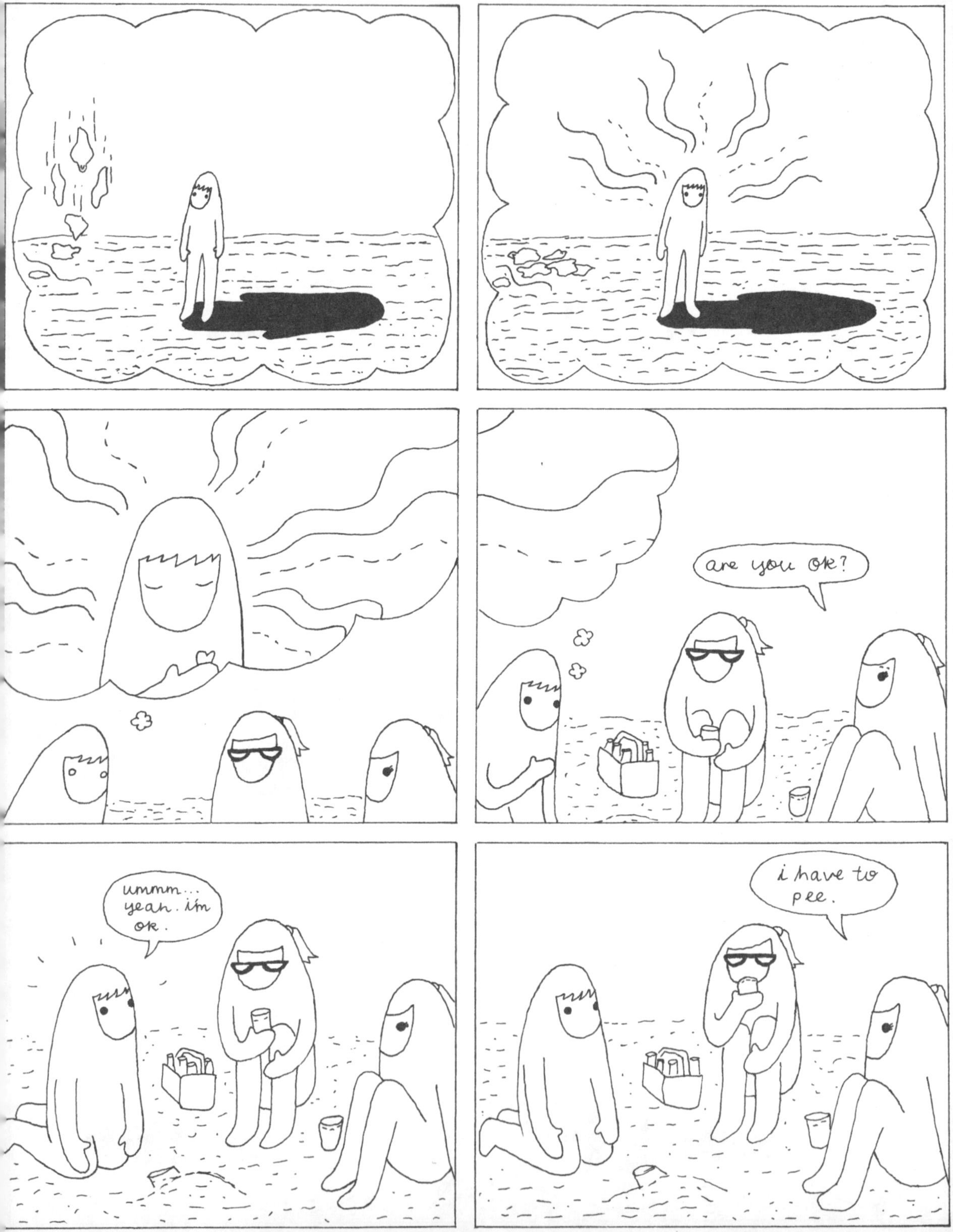
are you ok?
ummm... yeah. i'm ok.
i have to pee.

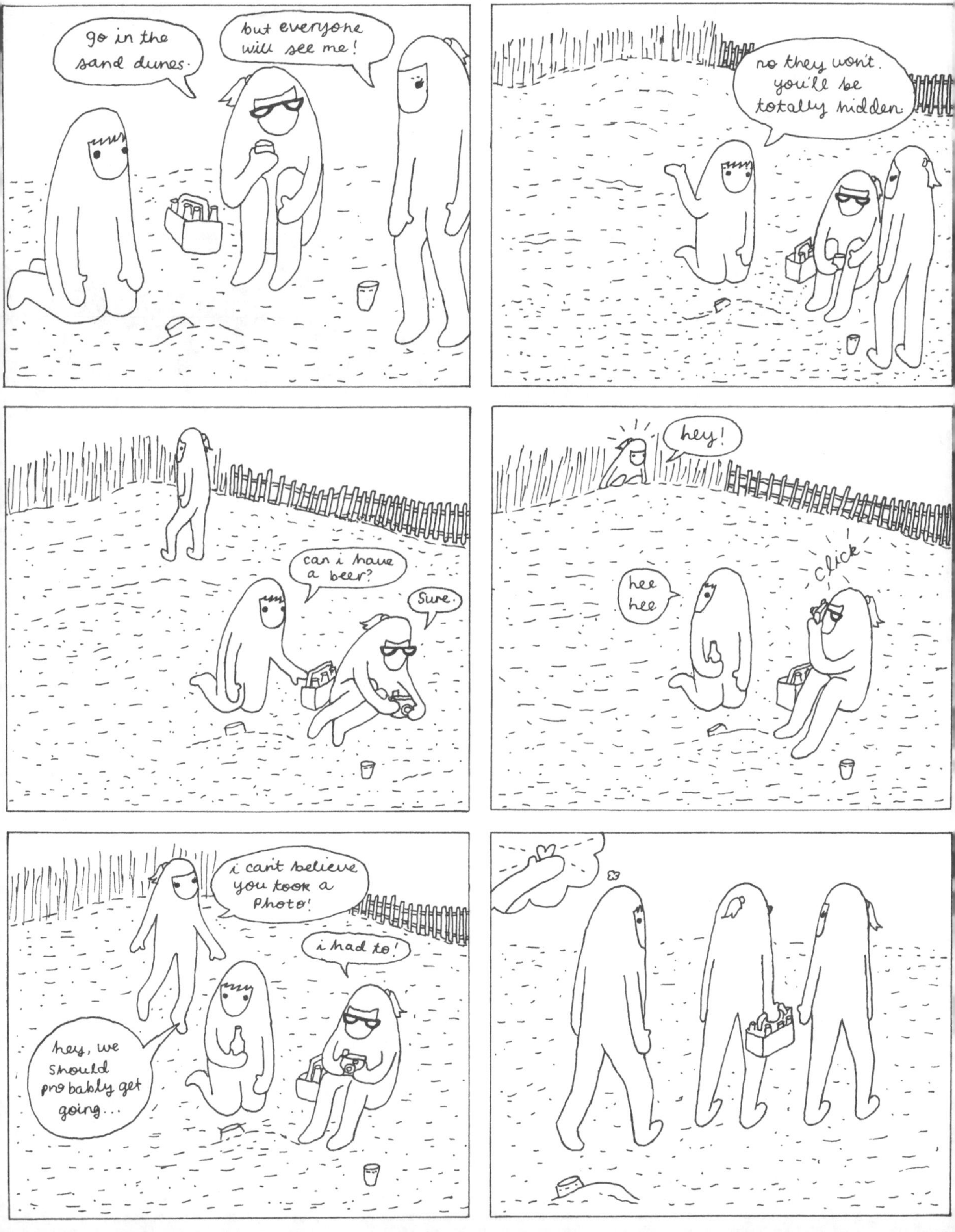
go in the sand dunes.
but everyone will see me!
no they won't. you'll be totally hidden.
can i have a beer?
Sure.
hey!
hee hee
click
i can't believe you took a photo!
i had to!
hey, we should probably get going...

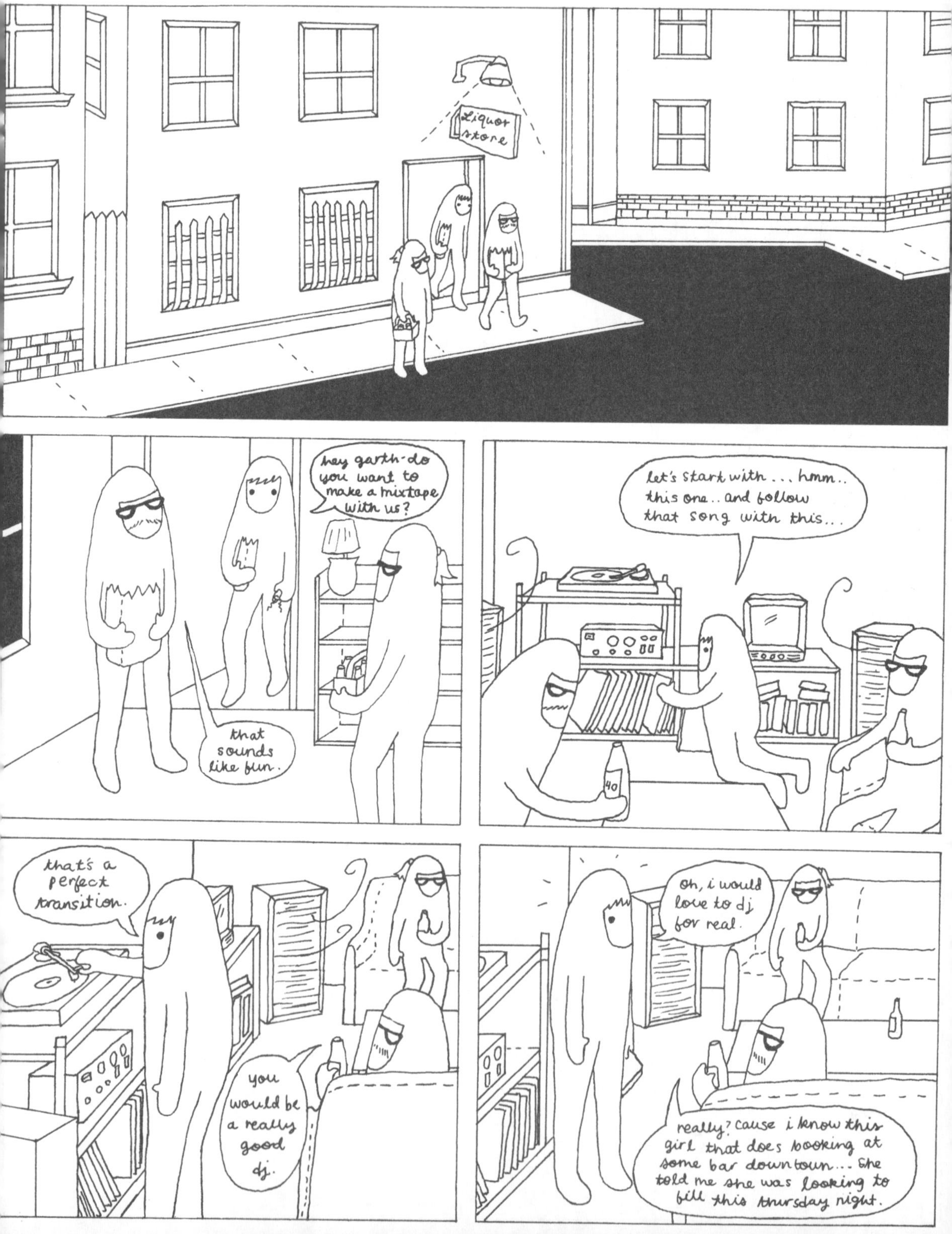
Liquor store
hey garth-do you want to make a mixtape with us?
that sounds like fun.
let's start with... hmm.. this one.. and follow that song with this...
that's a perfect transition.
you would be a really good dj.
oh, i would love to dj for real.
really? cause i know this girl that does booking at some bar downtown... she told me she was looking to fill this thursday night.
40

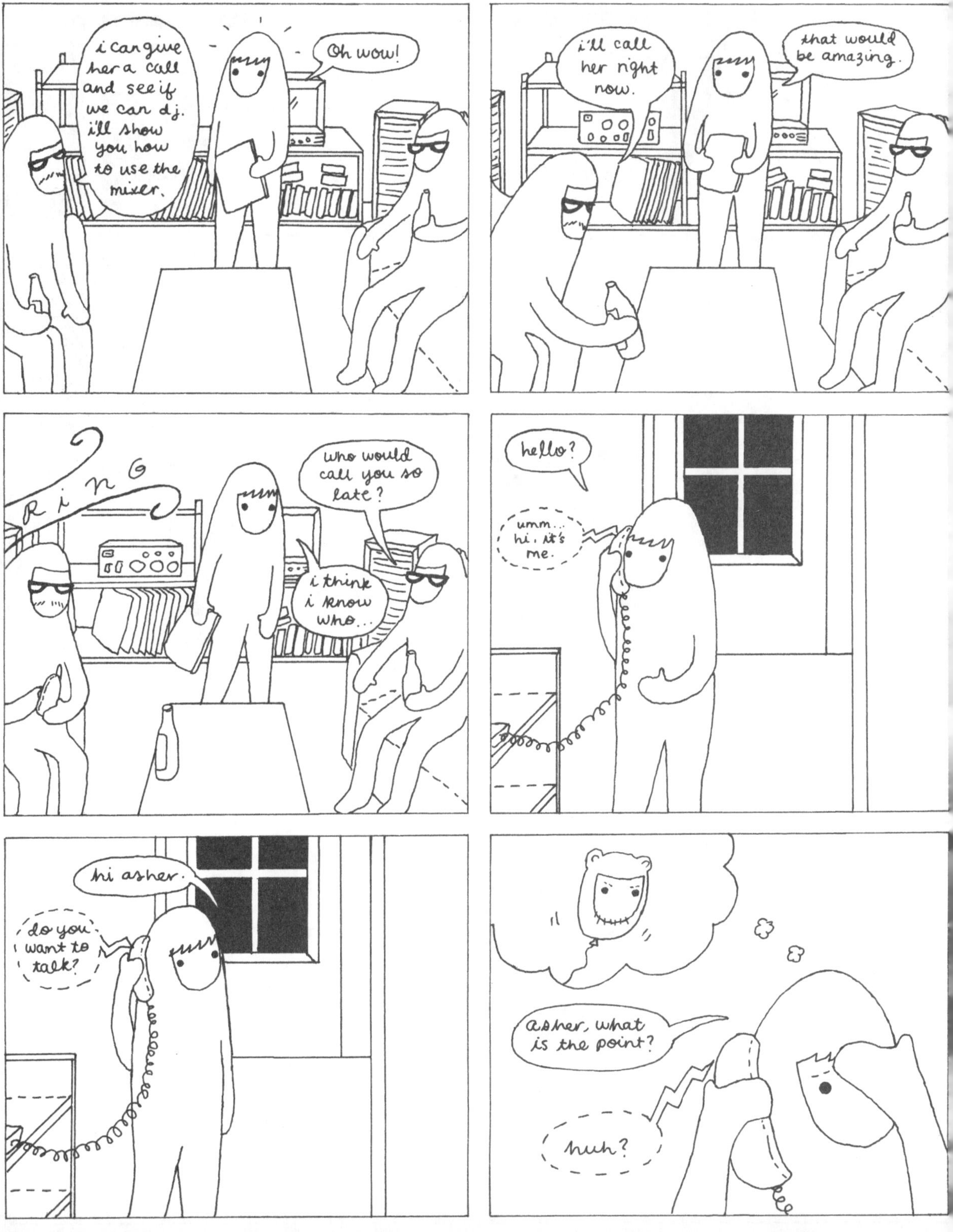
i can give her a call and see if we can dj. i'll show you how to use the mixer.
Oh wow!
i'll call her right now.
that would be amazing.
RING
who would call you so late?
i think i know who...
hello?
umm.. hi, it's me.
hi asher.
do you want to talk?
asher, what is the point?
huh?

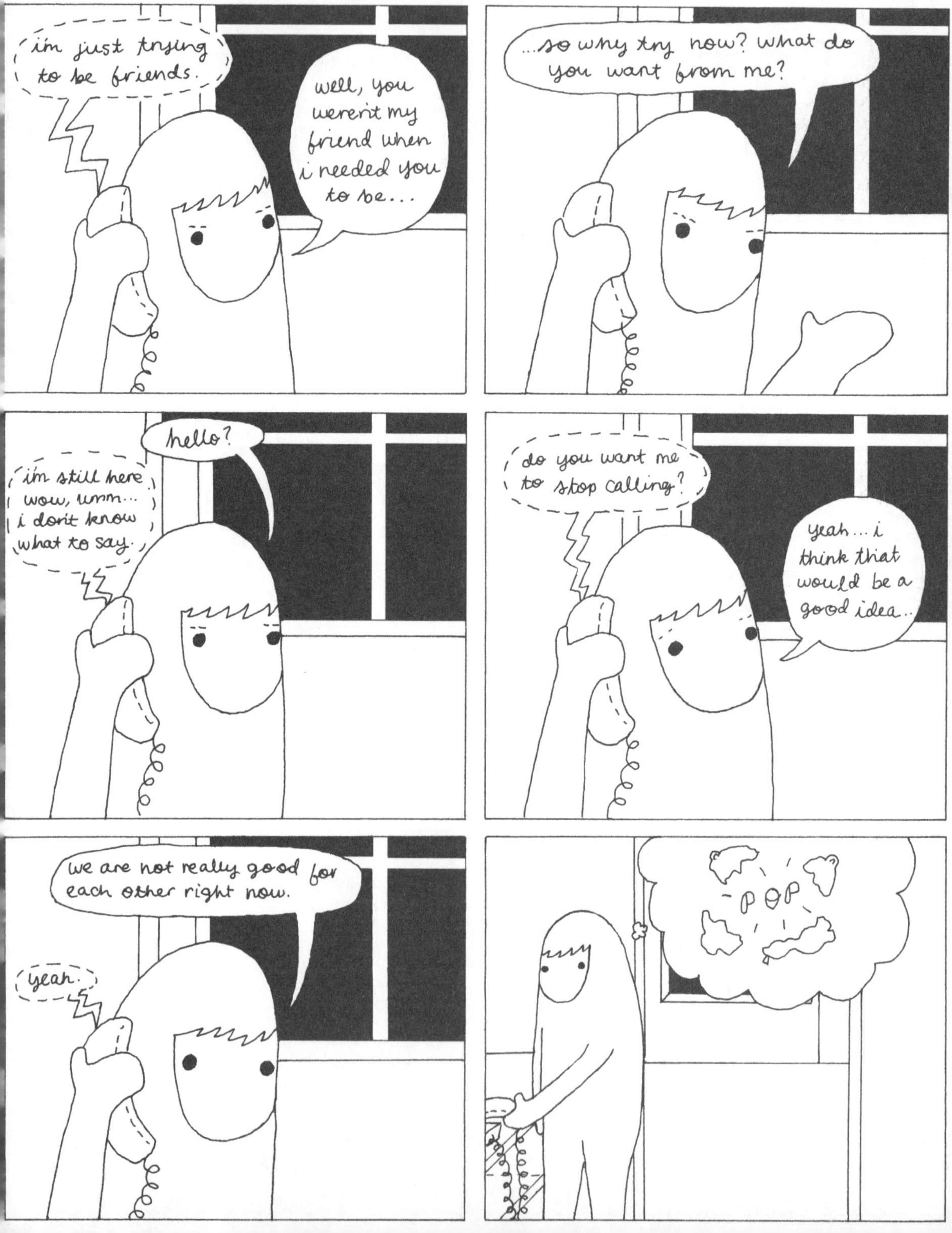
im just trying to be friends.
well, you weren't my friend when i needed you to be...
...so why try now? what do you want from me?
hello?
im still here wow, umm... i don't know what to say.
do you want me to stop calling?
yeah... i think that would be a good idea...
we are not really good for each other right now.
yeah.
POP

did you guys hear that?
yeah!
well, it's a relief.
hey, let's get back to that mixtape.
sigh

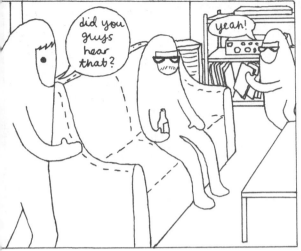

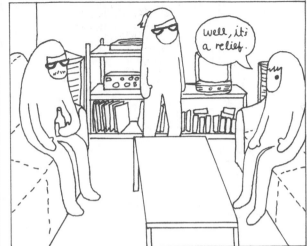

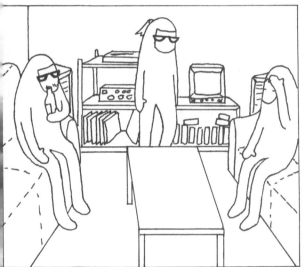

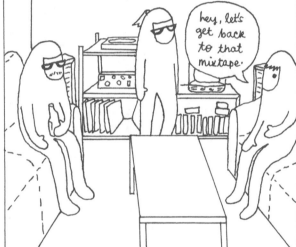

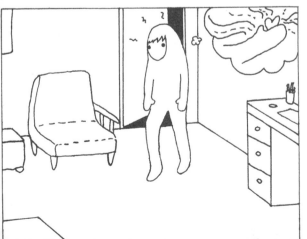

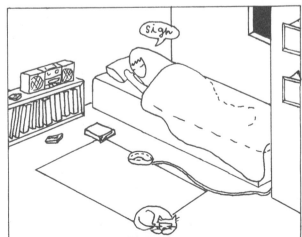

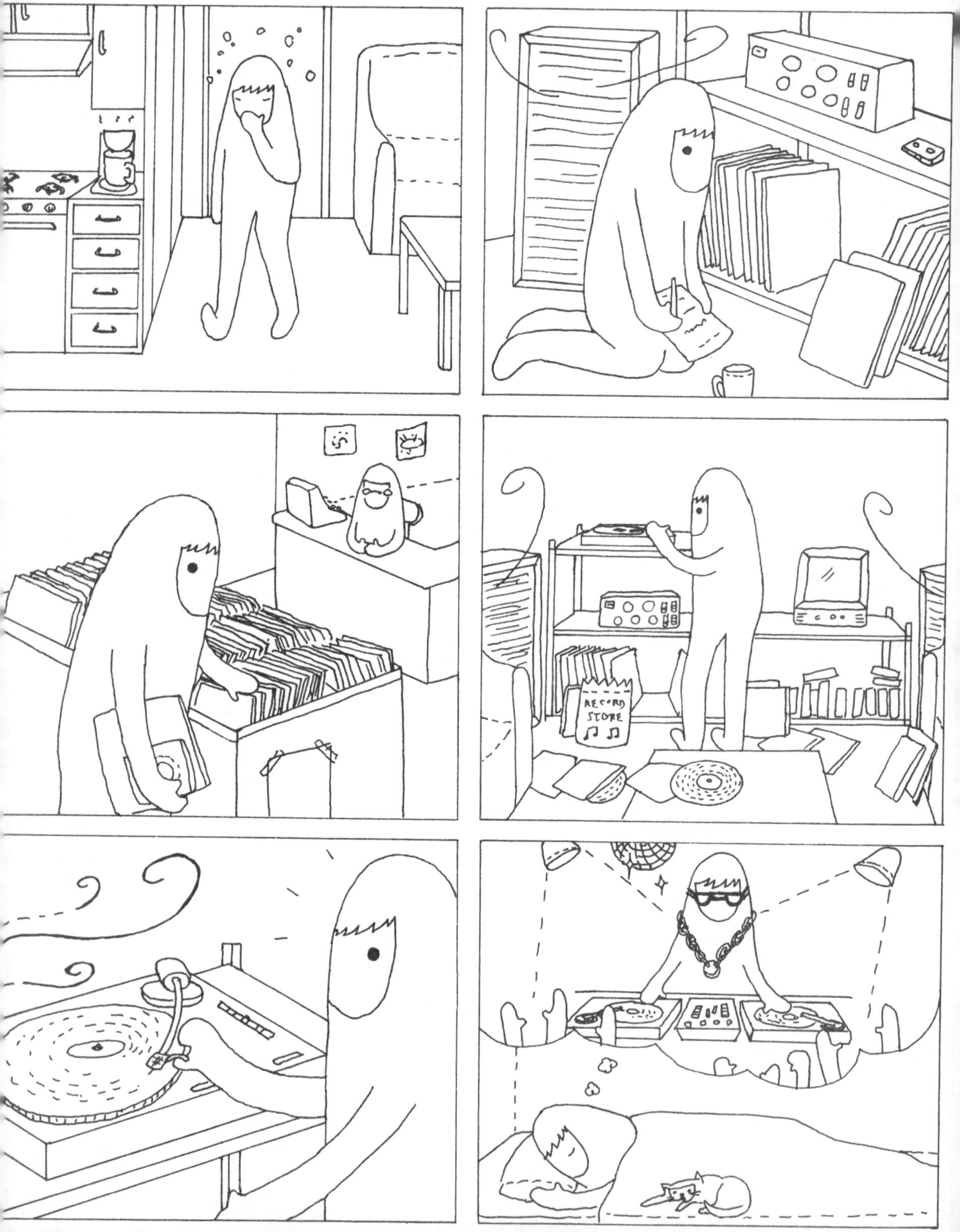
RECORD STORE

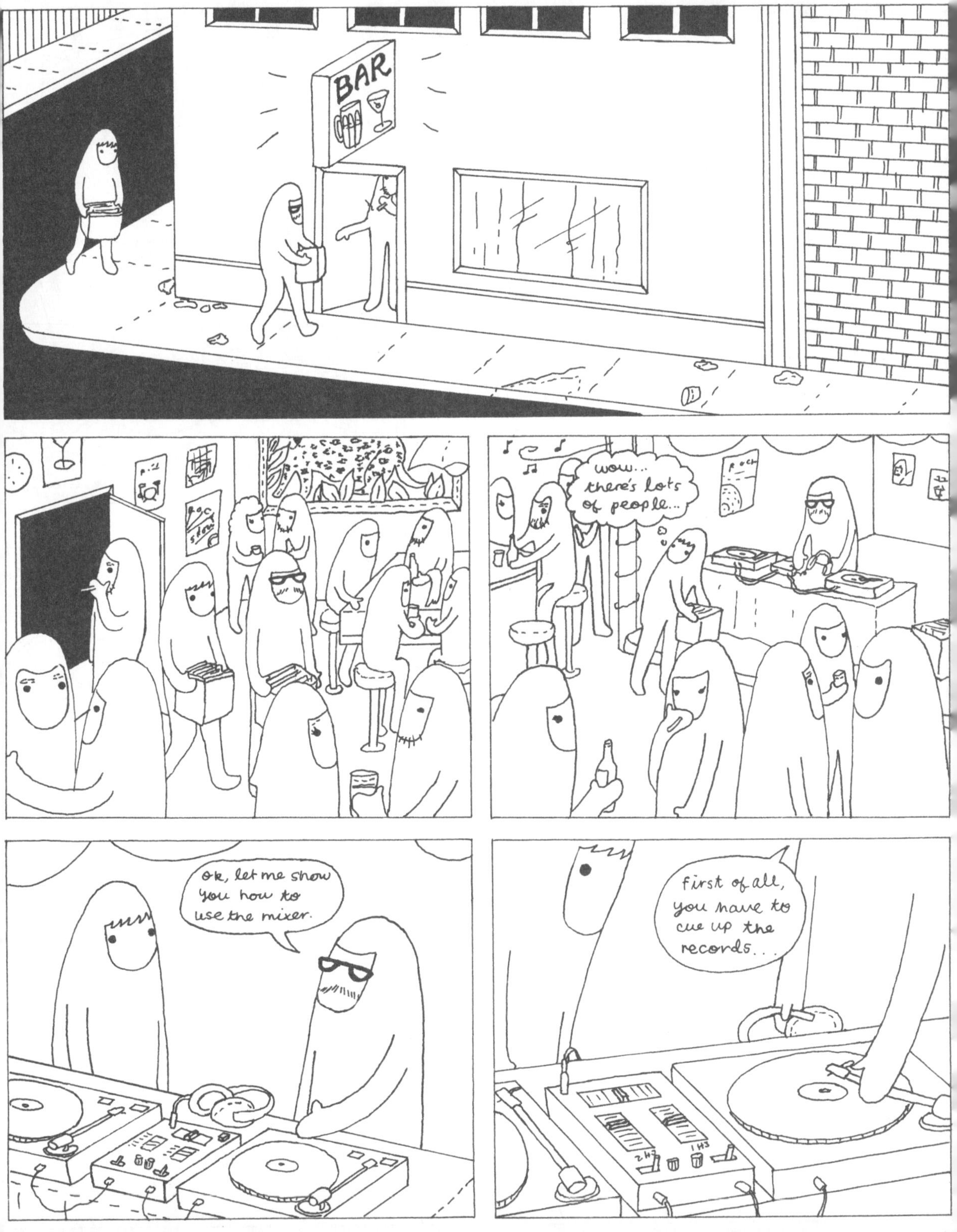
BAR
wow... there's lots of people...
Ok, let me show you how to use the mixer.
First of all, you have to cue up the records...

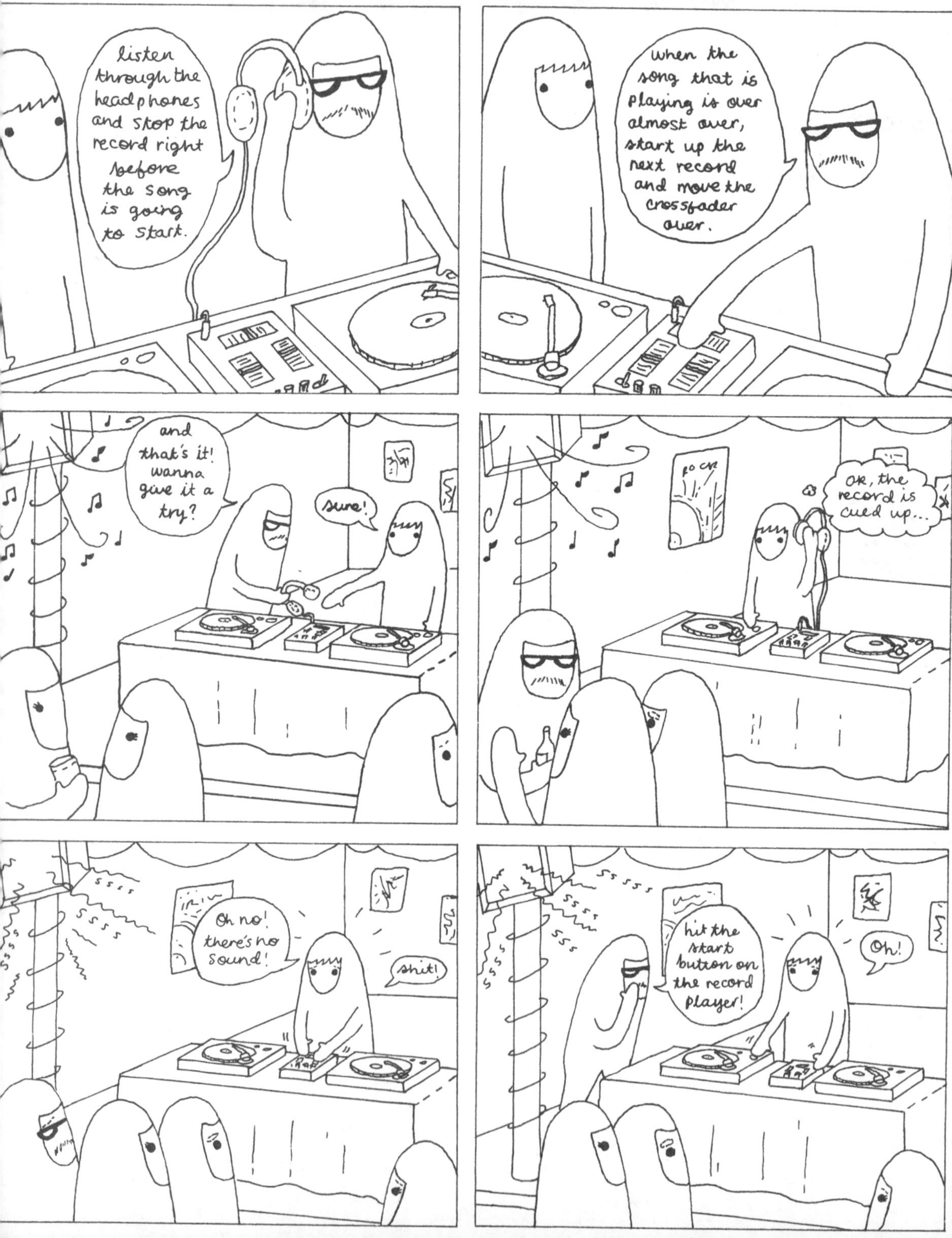
listen through the headphones and stop the record right before the song is going to start.
when the song that is playing is over almost over, start up the next record and move the crossfader over.
and that's it! wanna give it a try?
sure!
OK, the record is cued up...
Oh no! there's no sound!
shit!
hit the start button on the record player!
Oh!

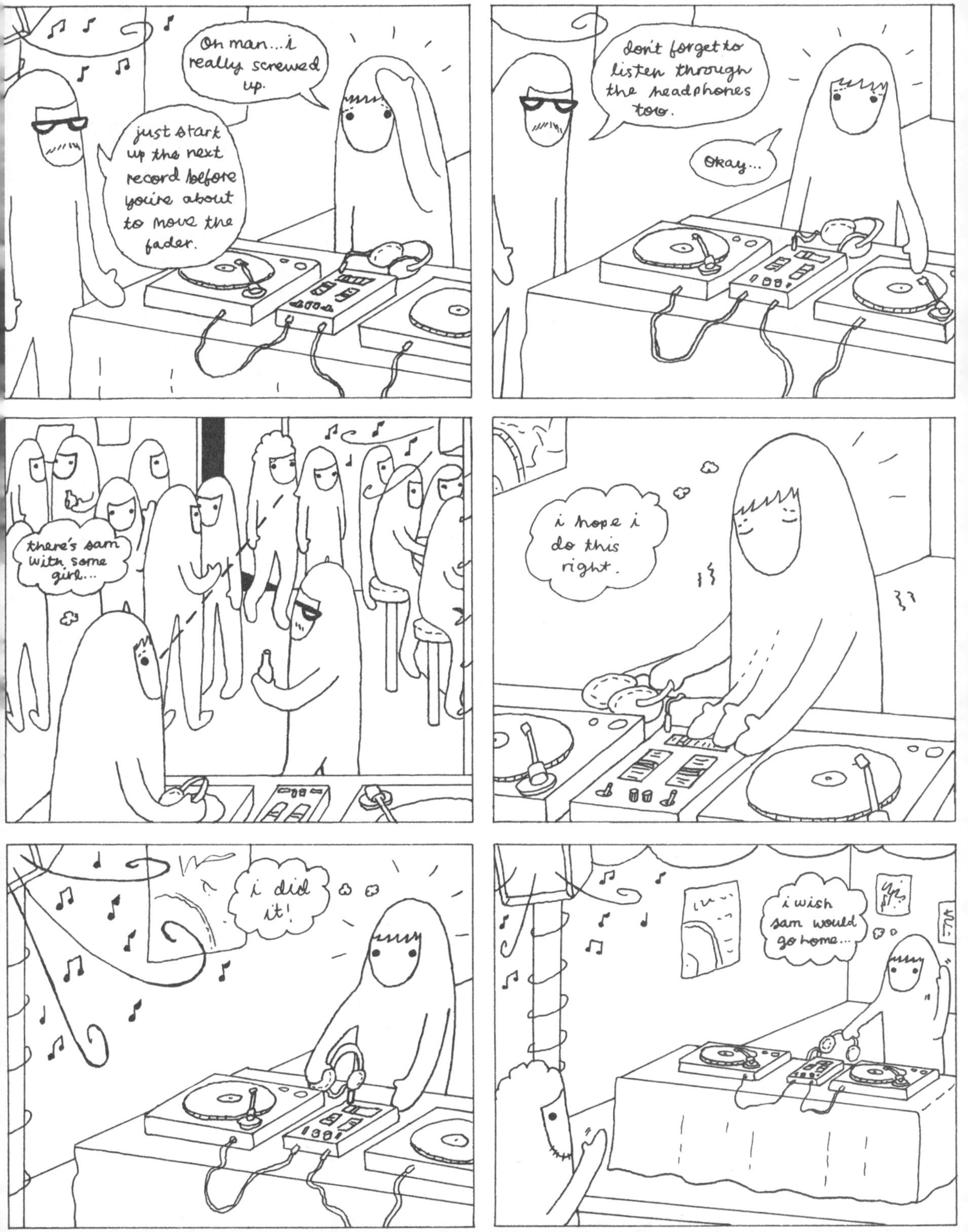
Oh man... i really screwed up.
just start up the next record before you're about to move the fader.
don't forget to listen through the headphones too.
Okay...
there's sam with some girl...
i hope i do this right.
i did it!
i wish sam would go home...

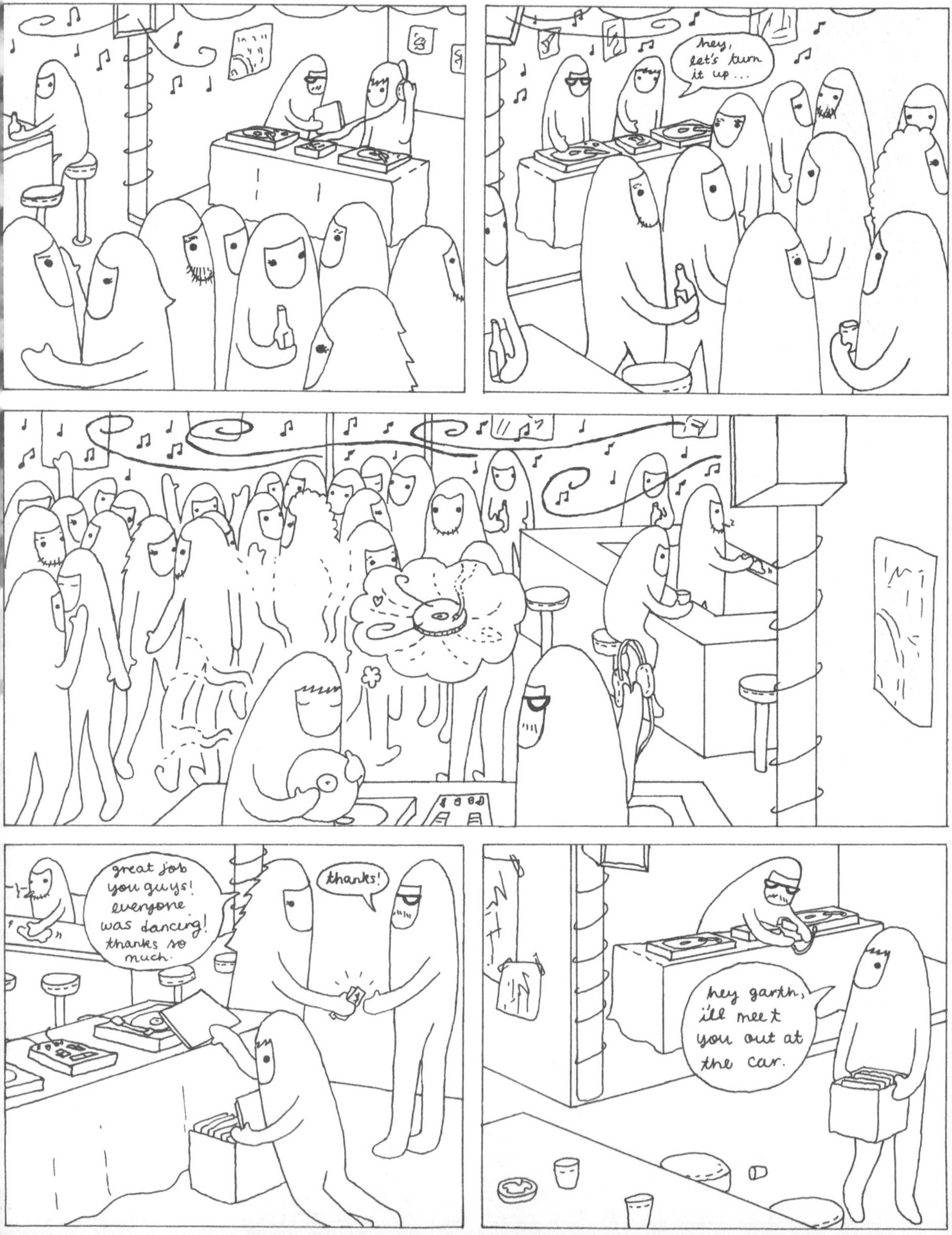
hey, let's turn it up...
great job you guys! everyone was dancing! thanks so much.
thanks!
hey garth, i'll meet you out at the car.

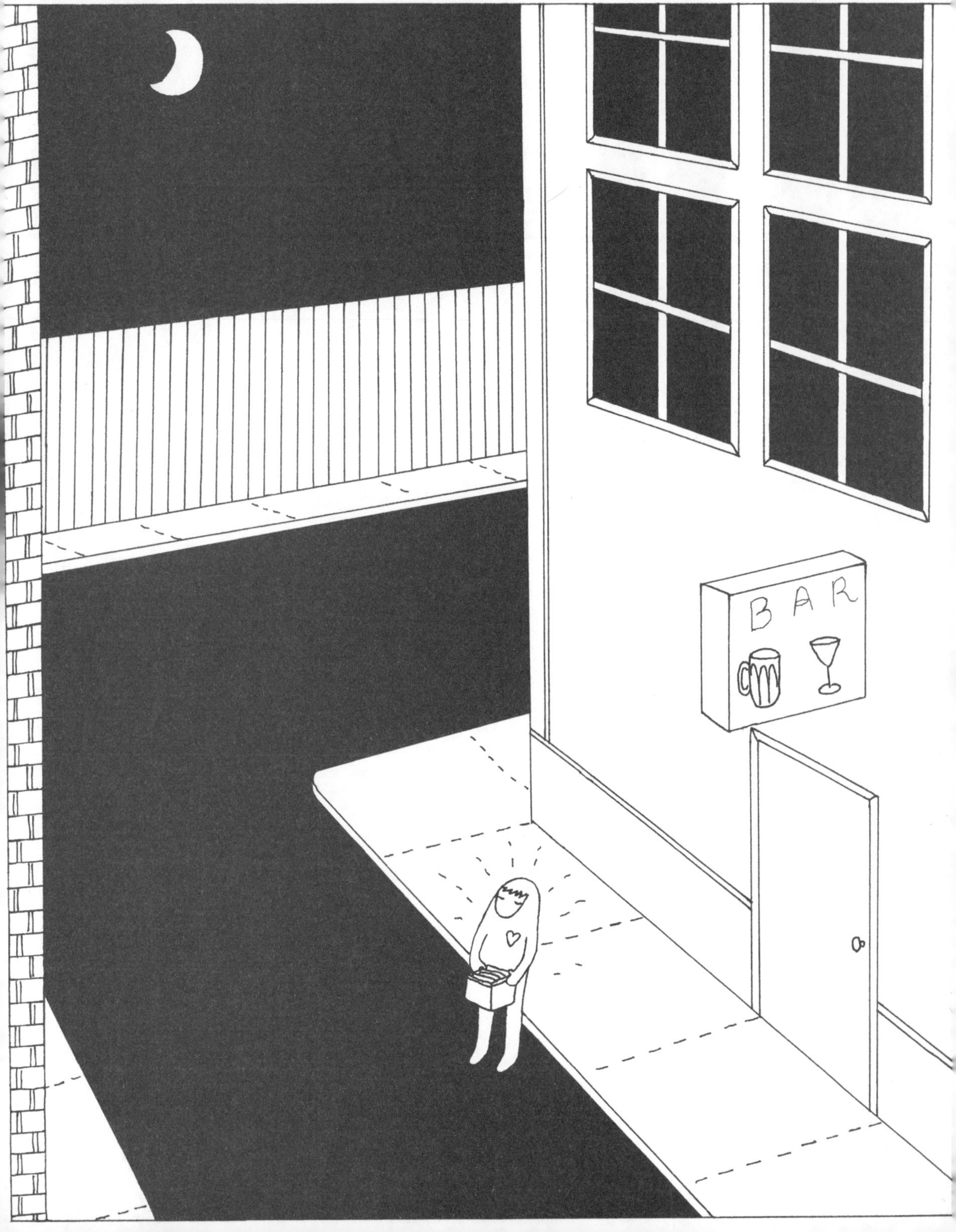
BAR

APR 2004